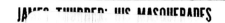

D1108051

1 7ch + 75ph
EE

DATE DUE

MY 10 '96			
JY 16 97			MY 18 '84
AG 6 97		85	
	OC 20 72	AP 10 '78	JA 11 85
			AP 5 '85
MR 23 73	NO 17 78		
JY 6 74	MR 9 78		
JAN 6 1975		AP	OC 31
			DE 12 88
JA 31 75	MY 9	MY 14 82	JA 7 '88
MY 2 75		AP 29 83	AP 20 '89
JE 13 75	FE 19	JE 15 '83	
	MR 12	MR 15	25 90
			JY 13 '95

RIVERSIDE CITY COLLEGE
LIBRARY
Riverside, California

DEMCO

STUDIES IN AMERICAN LITERATURE
Volume XXIII

☆☆☆☆☆☆☆☆☆☆☆☆☆☆☆☆☆☆☆☆☆☆☆☆☆☆☆☆☆☆☆☆☆

JAMES THURBER:
HIS MASQUERADES

A CRITICAL STUDY

by

STEPHEN A. BLACK

Simon Fraser University

1970

MOUTON

THE HAGUE · PARIS

LIBRARY OF CONGRESS CATALOG CARD NUMBER: 70-86882

Printed in The Netherlands by Mouton & Co., Printers, The Hague.

For Gordon S. Black

FOREWORD AND ACKNOWLEDGEMENTS

The first version of this study was completed three years ago as a University of Washington doctoral dissertation. My respect for Thurber's work was based on haphazard reading, and was somewhat chastened by the apparent exclusion of Thurber from the canon of American literature. I wanted to test my assumption that Thurber deserves the kind of scholarly attention paid to such writers as Stephen Crane, Sherwood Anderson, Eudora Welty, Flannery O'Connor and other writers of short fiction. So my dissertation was begun in what I hope was a spirit of interested objectivity: I would try to assemble a considerable body of Thurber's work in order to describe its form. And I wanted to know if this work would support critical analysis. This study attempts to describe the movement and direction of Thurber's work (I do not refer to its chronological development), and it concludes that the work more than survives – that Thurber is very good indeed. This conclusion was, in fact, one of the few aspects of my original version which was not affected during a year of revision.

Now, after two more years of studying and teaching American literature, I find myself even more certain of Thurber's ultimate importance. The value of this study, however, does not lie in my opinions about relative literary merit. Rather, I hope that some of the things I say will provoke literary historians to consider the specific relation of Thurber's vision to the uses of comedy by novelists and short story writers of the fifties and sixties. Perhaps a few scholars will come to agree with me that Thurber's work is the primary transmission line between the "native American humor" of the nineteenth century and the tragicomic fiction of such writers as Salinger, Bellow, Roth, Malamud, Heller and numerous others in the past two decades. Certainly, Thurber was almost the only comic writer of his generation whose fiction has consistent literary excellence. I hope that someone will soon explore the generic and historical implications of my conclusion: that, as Twain defines the "native" humor of the nineteenth century, Thurber defines the comedy of the present age. If this book is of use to such a future study it will have justified its existence.

I am happy for this opportunity to offer public thanks to people who have helped and encouraged me, most especially to James W. Hall of the University of Washington. Roger B. Stein, also at Washington, influenced subsequent revisions by his thoughtful comments on the first version. And Bickford Sylvester, of the University of British Columbia, offered many helpful suggestions during the first stages of this work. Finally, Mrs. Helen Thurber has given me invaluable assistance in assembling the copyright information included in my footnotes; she has my warmest thanks.

Two parts of this book have already appeared in print in slightly different forms. Much of Chapter I is reprinted with permission of the copyright owner, The Regents of the University of Wisconsin, from *Wisconsin Studies in Contemporary Literature,* V, No. 3 (Autumn, 1964), The University of Wisconsin Press. Its title, at that time, was "The Claw of the Sea-Puss: James Thurber's Sense of Experience." Most of Chapter Four appeared as "Thurber's Education for Hard Times" in *The University Review,* XXXII, No. 3 (Summer, 1966). I am grateful to the copyright owners for permission to reprint.

It is my pleasure to thank the President and the President's Committee of Simon Fraser University for a Research and Publication grant; I am most grateful for this assistance.

Since I was not married when I wrote this book it is difficult to follow scholarly convention and acknowledge my least expressible debt to my wife; nevertheless, I am generally grateful to her.

Whatever merit there may be in this book is due – far more

than they can know – to other scholars, especially those named above. None of them, however, is responsible for any errors or inadequacies of judgment.

North Vancouver, B.C., August, 1967   SAB

CONTENTS

INTRODUCTION

By the turn of this century, the disillusionment which accompanied all the manifestations of progress had begun to influence the new generation of writers – those who became the "naturalists". The boast of these writers seemed to be: I know that the dream of democracy has foundered, that man is trapped in a hostile universe – and what's more, I'm proud of my disillusionment for it proves my awareness of reality. Being alive was a grimly serious thing; comedy, under these circumstances, seemed almost an impudent repudiation of the newly discovered uncertainty, like Tom Sawyer telling Huck Finn that stealing a slave is a lark.

What little comedy existed then seems to support this view. According to Norris W. Yates, such humorists as John Kendrick Bangs, George Ade, Mr. Dooley, Kin Hubbard, Will Rogers, Irvin S. Cobb, and others, believed, in varying degrees, in " 'the reality, certainty, and eternity of moral values' ", were somewhat suspicious of "progress", and were fully prepared to throw out " 'polite manners, respect for traditional learning, appreciation of the arts, and above all an informed and devoted love of standard literature' ".[1] (In the second and third of these articles of faith, their views were faint reflections of the serious writers – Crane, Norris, and Dreiser, for example.) Their comedy seemed to be the last vestige of "Native" humor, so crippled and deformed that it inspired a host of articles with such titles as "The Passing of the American Comic", "Is American Humor Declining?", "Slump in Humor", "A Retrospect on American Hu-

[1] Norris Yates, *The American Humorist* (Ames, Iowa, Iowa State University Press, 1964), pp. 137-139.

mor", etc.[2] Furthermore, comedy must have seemed insignificant because of the appalling mediocrity of these humorists.

There was another and more talented group consisting of Gelett Burgess, Oliver Herford, Carolyn Wells, Peter Newell, and Josephine Dodge Daskam, called by Hamlin Hill, "The Purple Cow School":

[It was] concerned with pure nonsense. Flip, facile poetry was its major stock-in-trade, slick magazines and Burgess's *The Lark* its outlet, and Lewis Carroll or Edward Lear at least a part of its ancestry. It carried whimsy to the verge of the irrational, and its importance in the line of development for modern humor lay precisely in its tendency to invert, to peer inward into a fantasy world, to play with language – always for fun, but in ways that provided a groundwork for later ramifications.[3]

The linguistic brilliance of these writers is evident in the following piece of froth by Robert Williams Wood, "The Tern. The Turnip":

> To tell the Turnip from the Tern,
> A thing which everyone should learn,
> Observe the Tern up in the air,
> See how he turns, and now compare
> Him with this in-ert veg-et-able,
> For he is rooted to the spot,
> While as we see, the Tern is not:
> He is not always doomed to be
> Thus bound to earth e-tern-ally
> For "cooked to a tern" may be inferred
> To change the Turnip to a bird.
> Observe the Turnip in the Pot.
> The Tern is glad that he is not![4]

But no significant literature can exist which does not reflect somewhat more directly the problems of man and society. By the 1920's, when comedy again emerges as a full-blown aspect of literature, it seems confused as to the direction it will take. In Faulkner's novels, comedy recalls the 'native' humor of the nine-

---

[2] Hamlin Hill, "Modern American Humor", *College English* (December, 1963), p. 172.

[3] Hill, pp. 172-173.

[4] Hill, p. 173.

teenth century – Sut Lovingood, Longstreet, or Thorpe. Again, there is a comedy which reminds us of Melville's *The Confidence-Man* in its bleak diagnosis of the human condition, its despair over the failure of illusions and institutions. Nathanael West's *Miss Lonelyhearts* may be the best of these; in it, the unconfident confidence-man reappears, the butt of painful comedy at its most agonizing. As with *The Confidence-Man,* we never know whether to laugh or cry at Miss Lonelyhearts's pratfalls.

The direction West takes would seem to lead, not to comedy, but to an asylum. Concomitant with the recognition that our illusions have failed is, apparently, the need to construct new and more durable means for living with what Thurber calls "the Awful". Yet new defenses have to be constructed on a solid awareness of what the human condition presently is. A third direction in which comedy has developed is the line taken by Benchley, White, Perelman, and of course Thurber – the *New Yorker* group.

The "new" comedy is strikingly different from that of the nineteenth century. Where the earlier generations were either smugly contented with middle-class values, or were despairing at ever changing the external circumstances which were responsible for things being as they were, the newer comedians turned their backs on society to seek out the individual, suggesting that the private ordering of experience can make one less vulnerable to external forces, less subject to the despair and disillusionment which cripple those who depend on public illusions and institutions. Thus, the position of the new comedy is somewhere between those of "native" humor and "bitter" humor. The basic elements of Irving's comedy are present in Thurber; there is a fundamental similarity between the desires and fantasies of Walter Mitty and Ichabod Crane. But Thurber does not share Irving's contempt for the effete "intellectual" schoolmaster – a contempt which implies an affirmation of middle-class values. Thurber, rather, identifies with Mitty, or at least with Mitty's plight, and is somewhat reluctant to affirm any abstract values. Yet Thurber's very lack of commitment saves him, for the most part, from the bitterness of Melville or the disillusionment of the later Twain. What we have in Thurber is neither the easy optimism nor the bleak despair.

He admonishes us neither to "look back in anger or forward in fear, but around in awareness".[5]

If we are not to be crippled by our awareness, nor confounded by our inability to revitalize the old illusions, we can save ourselves by combining awareness with laughter. Henry Adams defined the failure of the past and hopelessness of the future in terms very much like Thurber's: both blame the industrialization and consequent specialization of the modern world for the present predicament; both see the result as either the dehumanization of the species, or the withdrawal of the individual from reality; both see the machine as a symbol for "twentieth century multiplicity". The pervasive irony of the *Education* reflects Adams' inability to use his awareness to alter the forces of life. With Thurber, irony itself becomes an instrument for change: not that external conditions can be altered; but irony can enable one to accept things as they are, so that one does not waste himself tilting at the unchangeable, so that one's anger at external circumstances does not become self-destructive.

Thurber's uniqueness lies not in his outlook, for that is similar in many respects to the apprehensions of many of his contemporaries; rather, Thurber is almost alone in using, as a comedian, material which in other hands is tragic. In Thurber's world, the cultural stereotypes are reversed; the world is operated for and by women, and men are more prone than women to failures, frustrations, and neuroses. Confronted with these failures to achieve culturally imposed ideals, men must throw themselves into conflict with women, whom they identify as the sources, or at least the agents, of power; furthermore, this is a conflict in which men must inevitably fail, and the result is a generalized ineffectuality. "Even a well ordered life cannot lead anybody safely around the inevitable doom that waits in the skies. As F. Hopkinson Smith long ago pointed out, the claw of the sea-puss gets us all in the end."[6]

---

[5] "Foreword" to *Lanterns and Lances* (New York, Harper and Row, 1961), p. xv. Copr. © 1961 James Thurber.
[6] Thurber, "Preface to a Life", in *My Life and Hard Times* (New York, Harper and Row, 1933). Copr. © 1933, 1961 James Thurber.

The "claw of the sea-puss" is not only a euphemism for death; it is also a symbol for the certainty of failure which is our lot. Like a recalcitrant automobile, a bird shrieking in the night, or a generalized conviction that whatever is attempted will fail, the claw of the sea-puss is a constant threat to Thurber's little men. Furthermore, it serves to discriminate between the two kinds of people in the Thurber world. The Thurber male with his analytical mind would soon realize that the threat implied by the claw of the sea-puss is both non-existent and ubiquitous: that is, one wouldn't look for a sea-creature on land and obviously cats do not live in the sea. None of *The Others* – women, parking-lot attendants, cops – would bother to analyze such an obvious a- nomaly, and would regard anyone silly enough to do so as need- lessly making things harder for himself – and for his wife – than he needs to. The Others are intuitively attuned to everything implied by "the claw of the sea-puss", so that, paradoxically, they are not even aware of their intuition; thus, for them, no threat exists – neither claw nor sea-puss. But the threat is there, no matter where the claw.

Thurber sees the species as defined by its conflicts; men com- pete not only with other men, but also against the dominant forces in a society designed for the protection of women and children. No longer the numb paladins who casually brave romantic perils for the sake of a shadowy heroine, men are sensitive, frustrated creatures whose very sensitivity and intelligence render them vul- nerable and ineffectual. There is no escape from these annihilating conflicts except into the world of dreams, and as we shall see in Chapter One, the dream world often threatens equally certain destruction. Like Henry Adams, Thurber blames the past for its failure to give the present any useful means for dealing with experience.

To establish Thurber's view of the human experience, I shall examine in Chapter One stories which are rather more serious than humorous in tone. However, Thurber is a comic artist, and while his "serious" stories reveal a great deal of his outlook, they do not suggest very clearly the means by which he feels we can

come to terms with life. Not that Thurber has a system to ex-
pound. In fact, his refusal to adopt a system enables Thurber to
remain flexible, and if this means that living is chaotic and dis-
organized, it also means that he will not be destroyed when a
system fails. For Thurber, systems imply confidence games and
masquerades. In Chapter Two we will examine some of Thurber's
attacks on systematizers – popularizers of psychology who offer
pulp-fiction escape disguised as scientific theory, and individuals
who are so dominated by formulated notions of human dignity
or correct or incorrect behavior that they become somehow dehumanized. Thurber himself becomes a masker to expose these
confidence games, using parody to impersonate the "scientists",
the *litterateur*, or the journalist-narrator of "The Greatest Man in
the World". The fault of such people is that their way leads away
from, rather than toward, reality and a greater awareness of the
world. Walter Mitty is an exemplary victim of such confidence
games; he tries to escape reality into a world of popular fiction
clichés, but these clichés only emphasize the distance between
Mitty's self and popular masculine stereotypes. He is led not to
any comfortable escape but to the verge of insanity.

Yet masquerades do not necessarily imply insanity if the masker
has sufficient awareness and self-consciousness. Becoming a self-
conscious clown requires the knowing rejection of illusions which
attempt to ignore real limitations and shortcomings. A need for
dignity forces Mitty into a fantasy world in which his real self no
longer exists; but Tommy Turner (in *The Male Animal*) learns
to use masquerades as a means of accepting himself and the
world he lives in. Tommy plays such roles as the absent-minded
professor, the professional liberal and even the male-animal foot-
ball-hero, but each role is played with the consciousness that it
is a role. As each is discarded Tommy – and the audience –
comes to an enlarged awareness of himself and his relationships
with others. Though Tommy has cast off dignity at the moment
of becoming a comedian, he emerges at the end of the play with
more integrity – and hence more dignity – than anyone else. As
his illusions about himself and life are abandoned, the ability to
look at things realistically affords him far greater strength than

he had before. Chapter Three thus reveals a new aspect of the little man – his potential for using masks for his own preservation.

In Chapter Four the matter of coming to terms with life is explored in connection with Thurber's "autobiographical" writings, especially the stories in *My Life and Hard Times*. As with most of the "education" books in American literature, isolation and alienation pervade these stories of Thurber's Ohio during the first two decades of the century. *My Life and Hard Times* is, in one sense, comparable to such books as *The Education of Henry Adams*; *Huckleberry Finn*; *Winesburg, Ohio*; and *In Our Time*, which record the adventures of young men during a time of profound cultural transition. But in another sense, Thurber's education prepared him more effectively to cope with life after the war and the depression. Growing up in the midst of an unstable and erratic family, Thurber nevertheless maintains connection with other people, threading his way carefully between the lunacy of his grandfather, the delusions of his female relatives and the uncoping "sanity" of his father. He has himself learned to become a self-conscious clown who uses comedy to balance himself in a chaotic and unpredictable world.

Chapter Five examines Thurber's excursions into fable and fantasy. While these are important elements in his more representational work, their use in such a story as "The Secret Life of Walter Mitty" defines the shortcomings of Mitty's imagination and of his life. When Thurber himself adopts the fabulist's mask, he is thus enabled to give full rein to the imaginative qualities which elevate so much of his work to high levels of artistic achievement. Thurber is always concerned with the relationship between appearance and reality, and in his fairy tales he finds a form uniquely suited for such an investigation. These stories are apt to end in confusion rather than clarity, yet the confusion reflects what has been in the character's experience; paradoxically, such confusion leaves the reader with a more integrated and a clearer sense of that experience. Stylistically, Thurber's method in his fairy tales is continually to juxtapose fanciful and realistic details in a way which leads at once to comedy and to serious statements about the human condition. The best of these tales, *The White Deer,* may well be Thurber's finest literary achievement.

Norris Yates comments on the "blackness" of Thurber's vision, and adds that he "shows affinity ... with writers outside the sphere of humor who disparage reason and stress the maladjustment of man when he moves beyond his animal origins".[7] Yates suggests that there are parallels between Thurber and Sherwood Anderson, O'Neill, and Hemingway:

Being more cerebral than Yank [*The Hairy Ape*] and more inhibited than Hemingway's males, Thurber's characters find little solace in drink – though not from lack of trying – and their sexual ventures seldom get beyond wishful thinking. But they too are specimens of nature; one of Thurber's collections is entitled *The Beast in Me*, and the introductory quotation concerns "the beast inside, the beast that haunts the moonlit marges of the mind."[8]

One suspects that Yates emphasizes Thurber's dark side in an attempt to account for literary excellence by somehow vesting a comic writer with the aura of a tragedian. Thurber himself is vigorous in defense of comedy, or rather, tragicomedy. In a late essay, "The Case for Comedy", Thurber accuses "the modern morbid playwrights" of preserving "terror and tension ... even at the expense of truth".[9] In the past, tragedy was in a position to make certain affirmations about man and his universe, based upon ideas of order and meaning which, for the most part, are no longer acceptable. Thurber's argument is not against tragedy as a literary form, but against the imitation of tragedy as a vehicle for imitating modern life. Shakespeare and his contemporaries, Thurber adds,

are not so much expressers of their time as expressions of it, and, for that matter, aren't we all? The playwright of today likes to believe that he is throwing light upon his time, or upon some part of it, when his time is actually throwing light upon him. This, it seems to

[7] Yates, *The American Humorist*, p. 288.
[8] Yates, p. 288.
[9] *Lanterns and Lances*, p. 142. Copr. © 1961 James Thurber.

me, has always been the case, but it happens more intensely now, perhaps, than ever before. Moreover, there are two kinds of light, the glow that illumines and the glare that obscures, and the former seems to be dimming.

If playwrights tried to rise above their time "they would simply sink below themselves, or sit there staring at the blank paper in their typewriters". If art has a function, it is to hold up a mirror to mankind. Tragedy could exist in a more confident time than ours, for it seemed to exalt the nobility of mankind, and reflected public belief in an essentially stable universe. But now we can neither pretend that this belief exists, nor that the deeds and choices which once defined "nobility" are still admired in the same way. The "terror and tension" which were once part of the tragic effect are now attained by representing, not the noble, but the depraved and psychopathic, in man: man dehumanized.

Yet if man can no longer believe in his own nobility, he can come to accept the things he cannot change. The truth is that man is neither depraved and psychopathic, nor good and noble; the truth about man is composed of the numerous trivial details which constitute his existence, and which also provide the stuff of comedy. In the modern world, "the true balance of life and art, the saving of the human mind as well as of the theatre, lies in what has long been known as tragicomedy, for humor and pathos, tears and laughter are, in the highest expression of human character and achievement, inseparable". "Comedy", he continues, "is just as important as tragedy, and often more serious in its approach to truth." The truth, if it is true, cannot exclude the absurd or trivial:

A few years ago, in a movie about a bank clerk who stole a million dollars, crammed it into a suitcase, got into a taxi with his unaware and bewildered wife, and headed for an airport to flee the country, there came a scene in which he handed the driver a fifty-dollar bill and told him to "step on it". Now I submit that the wife of an American male of modest income would have gone into a comedy scene at this point, but the writer or writers of the script must have been afraid that such an interlude would ruin the terror and tension.

We can imagine the wife's reaction if this had been a Thurber story. The ensuing squabble would not only have been "true-to-life" but relevant and essential if one's interest were with the characters. The bank clerk acting as if he were a character in a movie is only half the story; the rest would be his reaction to reality's intrusion: "'Not so fast! You're driving too fast!' said Mrs. Mitty. 'What are you driving so fast for?'" There is no doubting that for Thurber, the important thing is the "humanity" of the bank clerk and his wife, a quality which is nearly obliterated by the scriptwriters' use of them as instruments to achieve terror and tension.

Like many of his contemporaries, Thurber tends to emphasize the absurd and unaccountable aspects of life; but where many noncomic writers base on this absurdity outraged cries about the meaninglessness-of-it-all, Thurber uses the absurd as the basis for comedy. Life may well be meaningless, and the future is undoubtedly fearful; but dwelling upon outrage may lead to evasion of the problems of daily life which survive McCarthyism and even the threat of nuclear weapons. Comedy, for Thurber, is a means both for making man aware of his condition, and for rendering life more tolerable. "Humor . . . is the only solvent of terror and tension".

Thurber is a comic writer precisely because his vision sees not only the brink, the bomb and the neurosis, but also the possibility for surviving; through comedy, man may come to awareness and acceptance of his world. Lacking either a system or the convenient blindness which defends the more confident man, Thurber's little men wander about frustrated and sometimes paralyzed by their complex perceptions both of their own motives and inadequacies, and of the problems they face. For such a man, no mask can sufficiently conceal the sources of failure; his only alternative is to increase his awareness of himself and his world, and to learn to laugh at both.

When an adequate biography of Thurber is available, it will undoubtedly be of considerable value in demonstrating the relation between the man and his work – a consideration not undertaken here. Certainly this relation is not immediately apparent without special knowledge which existing anecdotes, magazine biographies and "autobiographies" (such as *The Years with Ross*) do not provide. On the surface, at any rate, Thurber by no means resembled the little man of his fiction and cartoons. His *Paris Review* interviewers reported:

Thurber impresses one immediately by his physical size. After years of delighting in the shy, trapped little man in the Thurber cartoons and the confused and bewildered man who has fumbled in and out of some of the funniest books written in this century, we, perhaps like many readers, were expecting to find the frightened little man in person. Not at all. Thurber by his firm hand-grasp and confident voice and by the way he lowered himself into his chair gave the impression of outward calmness and assurance.[10]

There are a number of anecdotes which show personal strength and a kind of tough anger which are available to Thurber's little men only in their dreams. Thurber wrote an outraged review for *The New Republic* (March 16, 1942) of John Steinbeck's *The Moon is Down,* severely criticizing the author for his alleged sympathy with the Nazi conquest of Norway. One reader called the review a "slap in the face", to which Thurber replied, "I am sorry about that slap in the face. I didn't realize my hand was open." [11] A character in a Thurber story would have worried impotently about the novel's implications, but would also have been rendered inert by dim awareness of the problem's possible complexities, and would finally have written neither the review nor the reply. It does not require a very sophisticated psychology to understand that Thurber – in common with many of us – may have been ambivalently passive and active; nor is Thurber's psychology uniquely relevant here. Nevertheless, we must, I think, recognize that the process I shall try to describe in the following chapters unavoidably reflects what must have been close to the central process of Thurber's life. The movement from passivity to activity coincides with the movement through awareness toward acceptance – if you will, through self-awareness toward self-acceptance. That his work reaches very high peaks, and that it

[10] Malcolm Cowley, ed., *Writers at Work* (New York, Viking, 1957), pp. 85-86.
[11] "Correspondence", *The New Republic* (March 30, 1942). Quoted in Yates, p. 294.

maintains a remarkably high level of quality, affirms not only Thurber's talent but also the successful synthesis of talent with vision. Thurber's fiction stands in strong testimony that its author's vision was capable of powerful development – a development which ultimately survives, and ultimately affirms itself.

I

THURBER'S COMIC NIGHTMARE

Thurber makes a frontal attack on the traditional lies, which he partly blames for the present state of things, in some of his *Fables for Our Time,* and in a cartoon sequence, *The Race of Life.* The implications of the original "Little Red Riding-Hood" fable are that little girls are innocent, a trifle stupid, and very much in need of protection from wolves by honest, stalwart woodsmen. In Thurber's version, the little girl instantly perceives that "even in a nightcap a wolf does not look any more like your grandmother than the Metro-Goldwyn lion looks like Calvin Coolidge".[1] The little girl immediately shoots the wolf dead with her automatic. The moral, "It is not so easy to fool little girls nowadays as it used to be", is fair warning to modern wolves who might try to hide in sheep's, grandmothers', or Brooks Brothers' clothing. If the clichés about little girls were ever true, that time is gone; we need new myths to describe things as they now are.

The old clichés tell us that women are innocent, creative, cautious, interested in cultural things; they wish to make their homes sanctuaries to which their husbands can retreat from their struggles to carve a living from the world, havens in which their children can be protected from life until old enough to deal with it. Men, they say, are optimistic, analytical, protective, practical, aggressive; they set forth on the race of life with their women and children behind them, eager to see what lies beyond the next hill, confident that food and shelter will be found, but undismayed

---

[1] Thurber, "The Little Girl and the Wolf", in *Fables for our Time* (New York, Harper and Row, 1940). Copr. © 1940 James Thurber; copr. © 1968 Helen W. Thurber and Rosemary Thurber Sauers.

if they are lacking. In *The Race of Life,* Thurber reverses the poles of these archetypes.[2]

The family sets forth from its cave naked, wife leading with a smile on her face, husband dubiously following, boychild last, carrying a banner, "Excelsior", whose motto is belied by the frustrated anger on his face. In the next panel, husband leads, his face grimly determined, wife follows right on his heels; by now, the boy has discarded his flag. Husband is overtaken by wife and child as they race "Neck and Neck", until the "Accident", when they all trip over a stone. From this point on, the race belongs to the wife, who has now made an uneasy ally of the boy. (When the husband talks to "The Beautiful Stranger", the boy's expression is nearly identical to his mother's; later the boy is ready to hit his father over the head with a rock during "The Quarrel".) The wife's superior attunement to the universe is marked as she becomes "The Pacemaker", leading the others, by instinct, in the "Spring Dance". When they encounter the first danger, "The Enormous Rabbit", they all stop, momentarily taken aback, then escape by tiptoeing past it. Wife and child lead on at "Top Speed" until they must stop for the husband who is "Winded". The wife carries her husband for a while, then eagerly leads past a series of obstacles until they meet the second danger, "Menace", a Simon Legree figure. The wife steps forward, protecting husband and child with her back-thrust arms, and apparently deals effectively with the danger. In the desert the husband is dismayed to find "The Skull", but the wife pushes him past it and leads on to "The Water Hole". The husband is now the laggard, climbing cautiously down a cliff, his wife and child far beyond. Child and wife lead the flight from the "Indians". Again, it is the wife who confronts danger, "The Bear", and who is later "On Guard" while her son and husband sleep. At "The Final Sprint", she, of course, leads, encouraging her husband at the sight of "The Goal", the gates of heaven. By now one is tempted to see these gates – like "the claw of the sea puss" – as the inevitable doom that waits in the skies.

[2] *The Seal in the Bedroom* (New York, Harper and Row, 1932). Copr. © 1932, 1960 James Thurber.

Here Thurber's view of modern man and woman, as he thinks they actually are, is explicit. It is the man who sees the danger in running too fast down the treacherous hill, or diving into an unknown river, and who, at the end, seems dubious that "The Goal" is worth climbing that last steep hill to attain. The woman's attunement is not merely to a society dominated by protective conventions, but to the entire universe. "There is no sense in looking for dangers or questioning goals", the woman might say to her husband; "you can't change things and you're just making it hard for yourself." But the male is confronted, not only by evident dangers which don't seem to bother his wife, and not only by the myths which say he is courageous in danger; the male is also the little boy who sees his mother succeed where his father has failed. The message of experience is stronger than the demands of the myth: failure is the burden of masculinity.

In the stories I shall discuss, the failures of both men and myths are examined in closer detail. Thurber attacks the notion that women revere culture and are creative, and that men are analytical and practical, in "A Final Note on Chanda Bell".[3] This piece is a parody of literary memorials in which a critic who prides himself on his ingenuity recounts his relationship with a lady who wrote very obscure books and led a bizarre literary coterie. The narrator had originally attracted Miss Bell's attention by publishing an article in which he revealed "the subtle affirmation compounded of the double negative of her unmeaning and her unmethod". As he becomes entrenched in her circle he is alternately grateful for her attentions and horrified at his growing certainty that her reputation – and his career, as expositor of her work – are based on a joke. He began "to fear that she had perpetrated, in her half-dozen dense, tortured novels, one of the major literary hoaxes of our time and to suspect that she had drawn me into the glittering web of a monstrous deceit, in order to destroy, by proxy and in effigy, the entire critical profession". After her death he waits in dreadful anticipation the news from some editor that she has left a letter exposing the hoax. He keeps

[3] *Thurber Country* (New York, Simon and Schuster, 1953). Copr. © 1953 James Thurber.

his bag packed for such an emergency; meanwhile, he has "hit on a new approach to the works of Chanda Bell. I am trying to read them sideways".

Unable to give up his role, the critic keeps on analyzing what he is convinced is nonsense. Far from analyzing, however, he apparently creates by his exposition a meaning which the novels did not previously have. It is not his fault that this silly woman is a fraud, but he has, in a sense, made himself responsible for her as a cultural force. Part of the critic's desperation to find a meaning is due to a fear which grows simultaneously with his conviction that Chanda Bell is a fraud. The personal indignities she has made him suffer as part of her coterie cause him agony in retrospect. Beyond even these is the larger indignity implied in her mockery of the values which have meaning for him and other men of "the critical profession", whom he thinks she is trying to destroy.

Thurber's little men frequently have a considerable fear of women, based on the refusal of women to take seriously things that mean a great deal to men – and these things include sexual prowess, neurotic disturbances, aesthetic experiences, theoretical knowledge, as well as simple practical problems. In the seven stories, *Mr. and Mrs. Monroe*,[4] Mr. Monroe receives a series of blows, the first of which is caused by Mrs. Monroe's drunken silliness at a stodgy tea. She tells the other guests of Mr. Monroe's collections – Sudan pencils, towels, matchfolders – and in order to "cover" for her, Mr. Monroe makes himself a trifle ridiculous attempting to discuss his imaginary hobbies; finally he forces her to leave before things get any worse.

As we are given the situation there is no need for Mr. Monroe to be upset. It doesn't make any real difference whether any of the people at the tea know that Mrs. Monroe is potted. What apparently is involved is some prior notion on his part of the kind of behavior to be expected from the wife of a middle-class businessman. The situation deteriorates rapidly. As the next story begins, Mr. Monroe's "imperturbability [is] at the flood", for

---

[4] *The Owl in the Attic* (New York, Harper and Row, 1931). Copr. © 1931, 1959 James Thurber.

Mrs. Monroe has been abroad for some time and he has been reading a book on "God, ethics, morals, humanism, and so on". What is apparently a customary illusion is upon him: he sees his wife as helpless and himself as masterful. The blow falls that much harder when, meeting his wife at the dock, he discovers that she is smuggling in a dozen bottles of Benedictine. Immediately he imagines himself in court helpless against a snarling state attorney. Mrs. Monroe gets past customs with no trouble but discovers on arriving home that a hat box with three of the bottles has been forgotten at the pier. Mr. Monroe returns with great trepidation, first denies ownership of the box, then grabs it when the porters' backs are turned and breaks into full flight when someone yells for a taxi. That night Mr. Monroe reads to his wife from his book, "in a deep, impressive voice, and slowly, for there was a lot his wife wouldn't grasp at once".

There is more than simple irony in these, the story's final words. Mr. Monroe really believes that by comprehending abstract statements, which he regards as profound, he is demonstrating a certain mastery over life. The delusions involved are appalling, for they prevent him from apprehending reality until the instant that it threatens him. He does not seem to realize that what he is searching for is the ability to handle simple, practical problems, such as smuggling twelve bottles of Benedictine past customs – a problem ridiculously easy for his wife. He is caught between his desire, on the one hand, to be what he believes is masculine, and his illusions, on the other hand, which prevent him from seeing the world as it really is except at those moments when it is positively threatening. His wife's illusions (she apparently believes, for example, that no customs officer is going to accuse a pretty young housewife of smuggling) are helpful.

Mr. Monroe's subsequent defeats point in a similar direction. A bat in his room throws him into as irrational a panic as the prospect of spending a night alone in a country house. The arrival of moving men, whom he is supposed to direct in the summer storage of his furniture, results in his completely forgetting the instructions his wife has given him, so that decisions are finally made by the moving men themselves. As always, he sees so many ways in which mistakes could be made that he is rendered totally ineffectual. (Here is one of many instances in Thurber's work where people with more limited sensibility – garage mechanics, parking lot attendants, moving men – seem, like women, to be aligned with the forces of authority.) At another time when Mr. Monroe's wife is away, he toys with the idea of calling up an attractive woman whom he fancies has given him encouragement at a party, but at once begins inventing for himself a series of excuses for doing nothing. Failure is so much a part of his life that he does not wish to jeopardize his fantasies of victory with the lovely lady by encountering an actual frustration.

Thurber's women join together, on occasion, in their battle against a vulnerable male. When Mr. Monroe has been carrying on an affair with a "very blonde lady", Mrs. Monroe goes to the lady and tells her of an incident in which Mr. Monroe got himself trapped in a shower at a college reunion, and was rescued only after the university engineer had been called. The portrait of Mr. Monroe running about naked, moaning " 'Woo, Woo' ", is enough to end the affair. At the close of the interview Miss Lurell is consoling Mrs. Monroe for her eight years of marriage to Mr. Monroe.

Neither men nor women ever forget the power they have to wound each other. Because more is generally expected of men, they are consequently more vulnerable; and the fear that men have of women sometimes causes a kind of masculine solidarity. In "The Interview",[5] George Lockhorn, an eminent novelist, is interviewed by Mr. Price, a young newspaperman. Lockhorn is hostile and defensive toward his guest at first, and as he becomes increasingly drunk, we learn that he is afraid that his creative powers are abating. There is a good deal of anger in his periodic remarks about his wife and in fact he seems to be getting drunk to spite her. He tells Price that the only item about his life that he has not given out to other reporters has to do with "the game" – and he will not tell Price about that, either. But we learn – and

[5] *Thurber Country* (New York, Simon and Schuster, 1953). Copr. © 1953 James Thurber.

the reporter learns – that "the game" has something to do with the relationships that Lockhorn has had with his four wives – perhaps it *is* these relationships – and that it is something which they and he regard as degrading. No matter what "the game" may specifically be, it is something which enables Lockhorn not to take seriously the domestic values which are important to his wives. His ability to hold his emotions at least partially free from his wives is his weapon.

When his wife enters she immediately tries to stop her husband's drinking, and after a quiet, nagging quarrel, she succeeds in sending him upstairs to bed. During the quarrel, the reporter has silently applauded his host's counter-attacks, and his distaste for Mrs. Lockhorn grows as she reveals that she is aware of her husband's creative degeneration. This knowledge is her weapon and Lockhorn can escape this knowledge – and thus defy her – only by drinking. When she apologizes for a slip of Lockhorn's tongue (" 'Is love worse living?' ") Price smugly replies that the novelist was quoting Joyce. When the young man drives off he has not got the story that he came for, but he has apparently got something more important, for he throws away his note paper and then his pencil. To write the story of Lockhorn's unconscious repetition, in his most recent book, of a chapter from an earlier novel, would involve a kind of betrayal of which he is not now capable.

"The Cane in the Corridor" [6] also involves the matter of male solidarity, this time in connection with a very different kind of marriage. Joe Fletcher, who has apparently undergone a recent eye operation, is visiting an old friend, George Minturn, and his wife. The situation is not very clear because all three are very drunk, and none is making very much effort to be intelligible or to understand the others. Joe, describing hallucinatory post-operative mental states, seems at first to be tormenting George, who, according to his wife, is " 'too sensitive' " to hear of suffering. Mrs. Minturn tries to deflect Joe's attention, and when George leaves the room she confronts him directly: " 'You're doing it

[6] *The Thurber Carnival* (New York, Harper and Row, 1945). Copr. © 1945 James Thurber.

because George didn't come to see you in the hospital. You know very well that George is too sensitive to visit people in the hospital.'" Fletcher asks if that is why she didn't visit him either and she replies that George would have sensed it and have been upset. Fletcher answers, "'He wasn't so goddam sensitive when we were both with the Cleveland Telephone Company. He wasn't so goddam sensitive then. No, he was practically a regular guy.'"

The accusation is plain. Joe holds Mrs. Minturn responsible for transforming George into this mass of raw nerves who nearly had to go away to the mountains after reading *Sanctuary*. Joe presses the attack, intimating that he might be blind now, angry at what he thinks is a betrayal of friendship. In forcing George to confront the reality of human suffering, Joe tries to overcome Mrs. Minturn's overbearing protectiveness. Finally Mrs. Minturn tells Joe to go home, and finally George is sufficiently aroused to protest – ineffectually – his friend's ejection.

The people in this story are as dismal as any in Thurber's fiction, but the marriage is not untypical. Mrs. Minturn differs from countless Thurber wives only in the degree of her dominance, and George is distinguishable from Mr. Monroe or, say, Walter Mitty, only in that he seems to have neither illusions nor magnificent dreams into which he can retreat. Mitty's dreams are of course no very good solution, for they represent the classical evasion of reality, and also the very considerable danger that the dreamer may slip permanently into his fantasy world. This danger is realized in two notable stories, "The Whip-poor-will", and "A Friend to Alexander".

Mr. and Mrs. Kinstrey, in "The Whip-poor-will",[7] are a typical Thurber couple. They seem to have plenty of money, with servants and a country home. They occupy separate bedrooms and have no children. And Mr. Kinstrey has dreams. In his first dream he hears "a blind man tapping and a bugle calling and a woman screaming 'Help! Police!' The sergeant in gray was cutting open envelopes with a sword. 'Sit down there, sit down there, sit

---

[7] *My World – and Welcome to It* (New York, Harcourt, Brace and World, 1942). Copr. © 1942 James Thurber.

down there!' he chanted at Kinstrey. 'Sit down there, cut your throat, cut your throat, whip-poor-will, whip-poor-will!' And Kinstrey woke up." Kinstrey lies awake until daylight comes, listening to and counting the whips and remembering with some perturbation having listened to whip-poor-wills as a boy.

At breakfast he complains about the bird but neither his wife nor Arthur and Margaret, the servants, have heard it. He visualizes his wife sleeping quietly in her own bed, and recalls being chided about his nervousness: " 'It's a notion,' she would tell Kinstrey. 'Don't let your nerves get the best of you. Use your will power.' " Here is a fundamental difference between Madge Kinstrey and her husband. She can say "use your will power" because to her the bird is just a bird. Since she feels no conflict she can prescribe will power, because, paradoxically, she does not need will power to attune herself to a universe which contains noisy, night-calling birds. But to Kinstrey, the bird has some special significance, and its significance is so strong that, will power notwithstanding, he continues to have nightmares.

The next morning the whip-poor-will began again at the same hour, rolling out its loops and circles of sound across the new day. Kinstrey, in his dreams, was beset by trios of little bearded men rolling hoops at him. He tried to climb up onto a gigantic Ferris wheel whose swinging seats were rumpled beds. The round cop with wheels for feet rolled toward him shouting, "Will power will, will power will, whip-poor-will!"

Kinstrey awakens and begins to reflect: "I suppose, like the drops of water or the bright lights in the third degree, this could drive you nuts, Kinstrey thought. Or make you confess." He reviews in his mind past misdeeds until breakfast, at which time he is chastised by Madge for smoking before breakfast. "It was no use telling her he had smoked them before going to bed; you couldn't fool Madge; she always knew."

At least one aspect of these dreams is clear: Kinstrey seems to feel threatened by the alliance between women and power. The woman in the first dream screams "Help! Police!" and the sergeant tells Kinstrey, "Cut your throat." Again, the wheels – not only a symbol for woman, but also, the fundamental machine – becomes a cop who taunts Kinstrey with Madge's phrase, "Will power".

The next night the bird shrieks again and Kinstrey leaps out of bed in the midst of a "nightmare filled with dark perils" to shout and curse at the bird until his voice is hoarse. At breakfast his wife ridicules his tantrum. " 'I never heard such a spectacle – squalling like a spoiled brat.' " That night, before going to sleep, he tries to whip his will into dominance of the bird: "If I get to screaming at it, I'll be running across that wet grass out there in my bare feet, charging that bird as if it were a trench full of Germans, throwing rocks at it, giving the rebel yell or something, for God's sake." But his effort avails nothing: he dreams of an umbrella which becomes a raven clutching back at his hand.

When he threatens to kill the bird his wife chides both his fear and his impotence to do anything violent. " 'I'm not frightened, for God's sake!' shouted Kinstrey. 'Frightened or brave, asleep or awake, open or shut – you make everything black or white.' " For Madge things are. She tells him he is " 'fussing about nothing at all, like an invalid in a wheel chair.' " In his dream that night, the various wounds he has received from Madge and many of the threatening figures from the previous dreams merge. He is a child again in a hospital, and Arthur holds him powerless while Madge repeats her previous taunts and Margaret threatens him with a skillet. Madge is both opponent and referee in a tennis match. Kinstrey awakens and stumbles down to the kitchen. Arthur interrupts him as he is taking out a "long, sharp carving knife" to cut a loaf of bread. Kinstrey speaks to Arthur as if still in his dream. The next morning friends call and discover that Kinstrey has murdered Arthur, Margaret, and Madge, and then killed himself.

That the threats Kinstrey fears in his dream are real can be seen in the wounds inflicted by Madge. But the greatest wound of all – greater even than Madge's taunts of impotence – is the example Kinstrey sees of his wife going through life untroubled by guilt, by inexpressible rebellion, or especially by memories of past failures. His failures include the fear he apparently felt before "charging a trench full of Germans"; the impossibility of getting "used to" the whip-poor-will (as Arthur or Mr. Tetford at the post office had); his sensitivity to Madge's bullying and his inability to deal effectively with her. This is the primary source of neurosis in Thurber males: not guilt for forbidden thoughts and actions, but guilt for past failures.

Madge Kinstrey is such a shrew that a normal reaction to "The Whip-poor-will" is to blame her insensitivity for Kinstrey's crack-up, and to say that she got what she deserved. While this may be partly true, any accurate notion of Thurber's world must suggest that Kinstrey's problems preceded Mrs. Kinstrey. In a similar story, "A Friend to Alexander",[8] it is clear that Mrs. Andrews can be blamed very little for her husband's madness.

He tells her, at the beginning, that he has "taken to dreaming about Aaron Burr every night". In the dreams he sees Burr insulting Alexander Hamilton, and he identifies Hamilton with his brother, Walter, who was killed by a drunk in a cemetery. While neither the matter of Walter nor the nightmares disturb Mrs. Andrews directly, she feels their importance to her husband; she tries to comfort him, takes him to the family physician (who tells him his heart is perfectly sound), and later suggests that he see a psychiatrist. Meanwhile the dreams continue. Mr. Andrews sees Burr murder Hamilton, and then Burr turns on Mr. Andrews, himself: "One Henry Andrews, an architect. . . . Be on your good behavior, my good man, . . . or I shall have one of my lackeys give you a taste of the riding crop." By this time Andrews' fantasies have begun to impinge upon his grasp of reality. When Mrs. Andrews takes him away to visit friends in the country, Andrews is shooting a pistol at a target with his host. "After the first few rounds, Andrews surprised Crowley by standing with his back to the huge bulk of dead tree trunk on which the target was nailed, walking thirty paces ahead in a stifflegged, stern-faced manner, with his revolver held at arm's length above his head, then turning suddenly and firing."

As his dreams continue, Andrews again tries to practice for

[8] *Ibid.* Copr. © 1942 James Thurber.

his coming duel, rising before the household and borrowing his host's pistol. The Andrewses go home that night, and Mr. Andrews has his final dream, the climax of which is a psychically induced heart attack. Mrs. Andrews sees that his dead right hand holds an imaginary pistol, and that he has not yet pressed the trigger. She collapses wailing that "Aaron Burr killed him the way he killed Hamilton." Dr. Fox concludes that she is crazy, "stark, raving crazy".

Once again, the source of neurosis is in past failure, and in the conviction that failure is the masculine lot. In the early dreams, Hamilton (Walter) "hides behind my coattails every night, or tries to". Guilt plagues him for his real or imaginary failure to protect his brother from the drunkard in the cemetery. He fails in being unable to dismiss from his mind this old incident, to limit his perceptions to actuality. Fear of failure is involved in his exchange with Mrs. Andrews before his last sleep. She wants him to sleep in her room, but he takes her invitation as a threat to his masculinity: " 'You're afraid to let me meet him. Why do you always think everybody else is better than I am?' " It is the masculine part to fight duels, even against imaginary and invincible opponents.

Burr, of course, symbolizes more than just the drunkard in the cemetery. He is the symbol through which Mr. Andrews acts out whatever hostility he had toward his brother, the agent for punishing that hostility, and also that part of Mr. Andrews which wants (like the real Aaron Burr) to commit a terrible deed with impunity and be untroubled by feelings of guilt. Mr. Andrews, like most Thurber males, assumes an alliance between women and the vague, terrible power structure of the world, based on the apparent coolness with which women confront the same forces and elements which terrify men. Mrs. Andrews seems to her husband to be as immune to dreams as he would like to be. But of course this is another of his fantasies, for at the end, Mrs. Andrews is caught up in his dream world as desperately as he was.

The difference between her "craziness" and his lies in the world's reaction to their problems, and in what they will each do about being crazy. When Dr. Fox was told of Mr. Andrews' dream he replied, in effect, "nonsense". When Mrs. Andrews has broken down at the end, he seems to recognize at once what has happened, will probably get her to a psychiatrist, and perhaps she will be able to work things out. Men, though, are expected to be strong, to have a no-nonsense attitude toward life. The world seems less willing or less able to recognize the failure of men to deal with calamities, than the failure of women.

In Thurber's world, the difference between what the world expects of men and women is always a major issue. In their jobs and in their marriages, men feel the constant threat of competition. Men must be successful in their careers, which necessitates both conflict with other men and having a great deal of highly specialized knowledge. In addition, they are expected to deal with an enormous variety of practical problems, many of which involve the particularized skills of other men. It seems a little unreasonable that a literary critic or an architect should be expected to repair an automobile. But the world seems to be contemptuous of "impractical" men, and Thurber's men feel their "impracticality" as another failure.

Thurber's women are of course exempted from such feelings of failure, since no one expects them to deal with such practical realities as are represented by machines. In "A Couple of Hamburgers",[9] a man and his wife have been driving all day through a "slow, cold rain" and still have a long drive before getting home. They nag at each other, using time-tested weapons which they know will annoy. The wife hears a noise in the car's engine "like a lot of safety pins being jiggled around in a tumbler" and the husband immediately feels defensive, since it is he, not she, who should have been alert to the possibility of mechanical trouble. He replies that the engine couldn't possibly make such a noise, and she reminds him that when a bearing burned out before, she was the one who noticed it. They argue about where they will stop for a "couple of hamburgers", and the husband finally decides the matter by stopping at a "dog-wagon". They

---

[9] *Let Your Mind Alone* (New York, Harper and Row, 1937). Copr. © 1937 James Thurber; copr. © 1965 Helen W. Thurber and Rosemary Thurber Sauers.

go in but the wife won't eat in a place she thinks is dirty and returns to the car. The husband eats his hamburgers slowly and returns to the drive, telling his wife about " 'the damn fine coffee in there' . . . he knew she loved good coffee". He drives off humming a tune he knows will infuriate her. She grits her teeth for a while but then relaxes when she hears "the safety pins in the tumbler, again".

In this story, as elsewhere, the woman allies herself with the machine, against her husband. Its failure implies no threat to her since she isn't responsible for keeping it running; if the car breaks down she will merely have another excuse for nagging her husband. One recalls that Mrs. Monroe estranged her husband from his mistress by describing his difficulties with the shower and with other mechanical things. And again, in "Am Not I Your Rosalind?" [10] Ann Thorne tries to embarrass her husband, George, by challenging his ability to deal with a wire recorder.

In this brilliant and disturbing story, the effects of competition and conflict are demonstrated, not only on the Thornes, but also on their dinner guests, Fred and Lydia Stanton. While the women are upstairs, George discovers that Lydia, like Ann, played Rosalind in the high-school play, and he spends the rest of the evening maneuvering the group into the library where he has his recorder. His object is to set the women against each other by having them read the same speech, one after the other, into his machine. Fred is very disturbed by George's plan and tries to persuade Lydia to leave, but she won't and eventually they all go into the library. Both women read the speech badly, and each is convinced that she was much better than her rival. (Thorne barely conceals his elation when his wife fumbles the speech.) After the recording is played back, the Stantons leave. Lydia is furious with Fred, who spent much of the evening in embarassed silence. Fred evades her anger by complimenting her performance, and is reminded that he has again missed "that turn" in driving home. The Thornes, on the other hand, go up to bed happily agreeing in their ridicule of the Stantons. "Thorne jumped a step, caught

---

[10] *The Beast in Me and Other Animals* (New York, Harcourt, Brace and World, 1948). Copr. © 1948 James Thurber.

up with her, and they went the rest of the way to their bedroom arm in arm."

Thorne's motive in setting the women against each other is fairly clear. Throughout the evening he and Ann have bickered, hitting at each other with favorite weapons. In forcing the recording, he has accomplished two things: he has succeeded, for the present, in allaying Ann's desire to compete with him by letting her have her illusion that she has bettered Lydia. Women, after all, are expected to compete only with other women; Ann is temporarily satisfied with her victory. But Thorne has not only gained bed-privileges (presumably) for tonight, but has also, on the wire, a weapon for future use. One sees their marriage as a series of more or less murderous quarrels, where equilibrium is maintained only by the knowledge each has of the other's power to wound.

But the Thorne's marriage is surely less odious than the Stantons'. Initially the Stantons seem a more attractive couple: Lydia does not nag her husband, and Fred's attitude of reserve seems preferable to George's bluster. But during their drive home, we see why Lydia has not nagged Fred. His capitulation to her temper has been so complete that she has no need to nag; he would not dare do anything to offend her. His earlier concern over George's scheme is apparently caused by the fear that playing Rosalind again, even for a moment, will make apparent the almost masculine will to compete and domineer on which Fred's fear of her is based. And surely Thorne could have chosen no better speech in the play than the one in which Rosalind, disguised as Ganymede, tells Orlando how she cured a friend of being in love by pretending to be a girl and alternately encouraging and scorning the friend. In the lists against his wife and the Stantons, Thorne has carried the day – at least this day.

II

PARODY AND UNWITTING MASQUERADE

In attempting to describe Thurber's sense of the human experience, I have emphasized his "grim" stories, and have perhaps obscured the fact that Thurber's importance is as a comic artist. While it is true that Thurber sees the human condition as bleak, this bleakness is nevertheless tempered by a margin of hope – that man may overcome the illusions which obstruct his view of reality, and may use comedy as a means of coming to terms with life. Thurber has warned us neither to "look back in anger or forward in fear, but around in awareness". A primary function of comedy, then, is to increase man's awareness of his world and his own relationship to the world; comedy must hew closely to the reality principle. An important means in Thurber's work for the making of statements about reality is the masquerade. In some masquerades, the masker himself is unaware of his disguises; in others, he consciously assumes various roles, perhaps as a deliberate defense against The Awful, or perhaps in order to try on a role in order that it may be rejected.

Parody, then, becomes a most important literary device in Thurber's work, since it is a means for the author himself to assume impostures. Robert P. Falk tells us,

The best parody ... differs from other kinds of literary criticism in that it breathes the very spirit of the style or idea it seeks to criticize. It approaches its subject from the inside, not from without, and will have nothing to do with academic yardsticks or arbitrary measures of literary excellence. ... Successful parody holds in equilibrium two opposing attitudes towards its subject – satire and sympathy. It involves an amalgamation of the satiric mood with a thoroughgoing understanding of the style it burlesques.[1]

Some of Thurber's parodies are explicitly literary. Here is Henry James:

If Charles Grantham's course, before the quickening wind of apprehension remembered and renewed, took him, as now, in fact, it did, straight to the high French windows giving onto the garden, if in the watchful eyes of his "lost" companion, his swift unerring progress took on the familiar shape of flight, it was all, he was afterward to protest, without the vaguest shred of plan. He found himself, nonetheless, within full view of the way out and it was but natural that our poor friend should, before casting anchor and reefsail, ask himself whatever in all the world checked his fair run into the green harbor and the wide free beckoning sea beyond.[2]

Or James M. Cain:

They kicked me out of college when I was about twenty-seven. I went up to see the Dean and tried to hand him a couple of laughs but it was no good. He said he couldn't put me back in college but I could hang around the office and sweep out and wash windows. I figured I better be rambling and I said I had a couple of other offers. He told me to sit down and think it over so I sat down.[3]

Or Erskine Caldwell:

A large woman with a heavy face walked into the littered yard, followed by a young man dressed in a tight blue suit. . . . "Who dat?" demanded Birge, peering into the dark. "It's me, yore Sister Sairy," said the large woman. "An' tuckered as a truck horse." The young man threw his cigarette on the ground and spat at its burning end. "Mom shot a policeman in Chicago," he said, sulkily, "an' we hadda beat it." "Whut you shoot a policeman fo', Sairy?" demanded Birge, who had not seen his sister for twenty years. "Gahdam it, you cain' go 'round doin' that!"[4]

[1]   Robert P. Falk, *The Antic Muse* (New York, Grove Press, 1955), pp. 9-10.
[2]   "The Beast in the Dingle", in *The Beast in Me and Other Animals* (New York, Harcourt, Brace and World, 1948). Copr. © 1948 James Thurber.
[3]   "Hell Only Breaks Loose Once", in *The Middle-Aged Man on the Flying Trapeze* (New York, Harper and Row, 1935). Copr. © 1935 James Thurber; copr. © 1963 Helen W. Thurber and Rosemary Thurber Sauers.
[4]   "Bateman Comes Home", in *Let Your Mind Alone* (New York, Harper and Row, 1937). Copr. © 1937 James Thurber; copr. © 1965 Helen W. Thurber and Rosemary Thurber Sauers.

However, we are presently more concerned with parodies which analyze not literature, but life. In "The Secret Life of Walter Mitty", Thurber's most famous little man retreats from the chaos of his experience into a world of pulp fiction masquerades. There, his failures and inadequacies are submerged beneath disguises which make Mitty a man among men; the hen-pecked husband becomes Commander Mitty:

"We're going through!" The Commander's voice was like thin ice breaking. He wore his full-dress uniform, with the heavily braided white cap pulled down rakishly over one cold gray eye. "We can't make it, sir. It's spoiling for a hurricane, if you ask me." "I'm not asking you, Lieutenant Berg," said the Commander. "Throw on the power lights! Rev her up to 8,500! We're going through!" The pounding of the cylinders increased: ta-pocketa-pocketa-pocketa-pocketa-pocketa. The Commander stared at the ice forming on the pilot window. He walked over and twisted a row of complicated dials. "Switch on No. 8 auxiliary!" he shouted. "Switch on No. 8 auxiliary!" repeated Lieutenant Berg. . . . The crew, bending to their various tasks in the huge hurtling eight-engined Navy hydroplane, looked at each other and grinned. "The Old Man'll get us through," they said to one another. "The Old Man ain't afraid of Hell!"

"Not so fast! You're driving too fast!" said Mrs. Mitty. "What are you driving so fast for?"[5]

With Mrs. Mitty's intrusion, Mitty is forced back into a world he cannot control – as he does the world of his dreams. But even there, his control is subject to the limitations of the clichés he adopts. The dreams are brilliant parodies of pulp fiction, and as such, suggest the extent to which Mitty has given over his own private imagination to what might be called a "public" imagination. This latter, paradoxically, is anti-imaginative, for it fosters the stereotype of the man without emotions, the man whose "voice was like thin ice breaking", and whose eye is cold and gray. Of course, Mitty is no such man; it is his private fantasies – his naked vulnerability – from which he tries to escape. The clichés lead him farther and farther away from life. The more he depends on the escape they afford, the less possibility there is of

[5] *My World – and Welcome to It* (New York, Harcourt, Brace and World, 1942). Copr. © 1942 James Thurber.

his confronting his real problems – problems with which he could perhaps learn to deal effectively. The increasing peril of each — dream seems to imply a weakening in Mitty's hold on life. In one dream he destroys his own attorney's defense by admitting (or rather, boasting) "I could have killed Gregory Fitzhurst at three hundred feet *with my left hand*." Again, he is about to leave on a mission flying "forty kilometers through hell". And at the end, he stands before the firing squad.

"The Secret Life of Walter Mitty" is tragicomedy at its best. — That it is an extremely funny story heightens, rather than diminishes, its seriousness. Because the author has set his parodies in a suitable framework, the reader too is allowed enough detachment to recognize the clichés for what they are. It is revealing to set "Walter Mitty" beside the first short story Thurber published as an adult, for we learn that he did not always know how to use parody effectively. "Josephine Has Her Day" was first published in 1923 in the Kansas City *Star* Sunday Magazine.[6] Despite stylistic gaucheries, the situation is recognizably Thurber's, but in its resolution we see that Thurber once allowed clichés to destroy his fiction as they threatened to destroy Walter Mitty.

A couple wants to get rid of a bull terrier puppy (Josephine) which they regard as a "failure". They finally find a man who will take it, but the husband later discovers that a neighbor of the man, the local bully, has stolen the dog and is mistreating it. When the husband asks why nothing has been done, he is told that the bully is "a little thick" with the deputy sheriff. The husband determines to get the dog back from the bully, and when he meets him in the grocery, offers him fifty dollars. The bully declines and taunts the husband. Here is the basic situation which

---

[6] *Thurber's Dogs* (New York, Simon and Schuster, 1955). Copr. © 1955 James Thurber. In the Preface to this collection, Thurber comments on "Josephine" as follows: "For a time I considered tinkering with James Grover Thurber's noisy, uninevitable, and improbable climax, which consists of a fight in a grocery store, but I came to the conclusion that this would be wrong, and a kind of tampering with literary evidence. Since I have had thirty-two more writing years than Grover, I would end the story, if I had it to do over, with the wife's buying back Josephine for the fifty dollars she was going to spend on a Scotty" (pp. xi-xii).

will confront countless little men in the later fiction. But what follows is certainly not Thurber. The bully challenges the husband to "come and get her".

"Maybe I will," said Dick. He was quivering slightly and his legs felt strangely strained under him.

"And maybe you'll get a clout like I've had to give yer damn dog now and again," laughed the man, brutally showing his teeth in a grin at his companions.

Things grew a little hazy in front of Dickinson – a little hazy and red. He realized, with something like a flash of fire in his brain, that this strange brute had beaten his dog . . . Josephine . . .

In two bounds he was across the room, for he was lithe and quick, if no match for the other in strength. Before Gibbs could remove one ankle from the other, as he lounged against the counter – before he could take the pipe from his hand, Dickinson struck him full in the mouth with all the force of a long right swing.

The fight that follows is straight out of pulp fiction – the Western saloon brawl.

The swoop of the oncoming giant was powerful. Dickinson turned and in sheer fright, ran to the door. But there he suddenly whirled. With a quick, mad, desperate movement he hurled himself straight at the feet of the charging form. . . . He struck the man just above the ankles.

Gibbs went toppling clumsily over him and hit the floor with a terrific crash. He fell near a newly opened box of hammers, glistening with blue steel heads and white-labeled handles. . . . Gibbs' throw was wild. The hammer crashed into an unlighted lamp high above the counter, and glass tinkled sharply as the lamp swung and creaked dismally. . . . Dick darted straight out at his foe, swinging the chair up from the floor as he came. Gibbs, somewhat startled, brought his hammer stroke down squarely on the upturned legs of the chair, two of which caught him solidly under the arm.

And so on for more than four pages! When the fight is over and Dick is afraid he has killed Gibbs with a hammer, who should arrive but – The Sheriff!

The crazy thought went through Dickinson's mind that this must be a movie. Then he fainted.

When he came to, he found himself firmly held in the arm of the law. His eyes widened and a question formed in his mind. Had he killed Gibbs?

"You're going to take a ride with me," said the sheriff grimly.

Dick shivered. "You and me," continued the sheriff, "are going up after that female bitch now. I like a man'll fight all hell for his dog, even if it *ain't* his."

Here is the little man's every wish fulfilled. Not only has he beaten up the neighborhood bully, but he has won the admiration of the law. It is Mr. Kinstrey defeating all the dark forces which inhabit his dream world. Or rather, it is Walter Mitty, letting the district-attorney "have it on the point of the chin".

But of course it is neither. By the time Thurber comes to write "The Whip-poor-will", he is infinitely more skilled and subtle. And it is not Walter Mitty, either, because the fight in "Josephine Has Her Day" is not presented as a dream, but as reality – and it is utterly unconvincing. When Dick thinks "that this must be a movie", he echoes what the reader knew long before. The clichés in which the fight is presented are false precisely because the author seems to depend on them. What Thurber has learned by the time he writes "The Secret Life of Walter Mitty", is that clichés are valuable only when they are firmly under the author's control.

In the next few years Thurber learned to control clichés through parody. When he returned to the United States in 1925, after a brief tour of duty with the Expatriates, he wrote a burlesque of popularized scientific books, *Why We Behave Like Microbe Hunters,* but was unable to sell it. By 1929, however, he was able to collaborate with E. B. White on one of the most successful of modern parodies, *Is Sex Necessary?* [7] The book spoofs glib popularizers of Freud, writers who had discovered sex and could talk of nothing else. The answer to the title's question is, as Norris Yates says, "yes, of course sex is necessary, but overemphasis and oversimplification of it are not".[8] In Chap-

---

[7] *Is Sex Necessary?* (New York, Harper and Row, 1929). Copr. © 1929, 1957 James Thurber and E. B. White. The authorship of the various sections of this book should be apparent to anyone acquainted with both Thurber's and White's work. Thurber creates comedy through incident, White through verbal wit. For the record, Norris Yates quotes a letter from Mrs. Helen Thurber saying that her husband wrote the Preface to the 1929 edition, and chapters I, III, V, VII, and the Glossary (*The American Humorist*, Ames, Iowa, 1964, p. 384).

[8] Yates, p. 288.

ter Three, "A Discussion of Feminine Types", parody is used
to establish a masquerade. As Falk suggests in his discussion of
parody, the subject is approached "from the inside"; Thurber is
enabled to hold "in equilibrium two opposing attitudes toward
his subject – satire and sympathy".

The chapter's opening sentence establishes the voice of the
"scientist", a pedant whose command of himself depends upon
the distance his "objectivity" puts between him and his subject.

In speaking of the weaker sex in this book, the authors usually confine themselves to the generalization "Woman", "women", and "the
female". For the larger discussions of sex, these comprehensive terms
suffice. Yet no examination of the pitiable problem of Man and
Woman would be complete without some effort to define a few of
the more important types of the female.

But Thurber is after bigger game here than the mere notion that
it is neither possible nor useful to categorize human beings. He
assumes the role of the pedant, and this assumption involves
sympathy and understanding of the man who could write such
a book. There is really a double mask here: Thurber masquerades
as a scientist, and the scientist masquerades as a scientist – for
the man precedes his occupation – and the scientist's disguise
slips revealingly from time to time. In his investigations of the
various "types", he tells of attempting to get acquainted with
ladies that he meets. A Quiet Type ("Q.T.") he meets at a party
intrigues him.

I stole glances at her from time to time, trying to make them appear
ingenuous and friendly, rather than bold or suggestive, an achievement rendered somewhat troublesome by an unfortunate involuntary
winking of the left eyelid to which I am unhappily subject.
. . . Steeling myself for an ordeal to which I am unused – or was at
the time – I moved directly to her side and grasped her hand. "Hallo,
baby! Some fun – hah?" I said – a method of attack which I had de-
vised in advance. She was obviously shocked, and instantly rose from
her chair and followed the others into the next room. I never saw her
again, nor have I been invited to that little home since. Now for some
conclusions. . . .

His misadventures extend to his investigation of not only Q.T.'s,
but also Buttonhole-twister, Clinging Vine, Don't dear, and Out-

doors types. Before many of them have occurred, however, the reader becomes aware that the scientist uses his mask as an excuse to make passes at young ladies – something he cannot do as a "dependable family man", and also as a shy and rather clumsy man. But, as the mask slips, the reader discovers a human being underneath it and sympathy which one withholds from the pedant is extended to the man. The very act of parody has stripped away pretense, and with it, the dignity attached to the mask. But the latter is dispensable. Thurber told Max Eastman, "Human dignity, the humorist believes, is not only silly but a little sad. So are the dreams and conventions and illusions. The fine brave fragile stuff that men live by. They look so swell, and go to pieces so easily." [9]

Thurber's attitude toward dreams, conventions, illusions and human dignity is central to the parodies we are considering. Walter Mitty sought to vest himself with these civilized trappings in his fantasies, but we have seen where they led him. In a series of comic essays, *Let Your Mind Alone!,* Thurber attacks writers of "success books" whose advice propagates these trappings.[10] Here Thurber brings the chaos of his world into the simplicity of the worlds described by the self-designated "realists", and concludes that man is better off if his mind remains flexible than if it is governed by a system. The "success experts" do not describe real people or situations; rather, they offer a form of escape to the reader, comparable to that offered in pulp-fiction.

In "Destructive Forces in Life", the second of the ten essays, Thurber quotes a case-history from a book called *How to Worry Successfully* by a Mr. David Seabury:

"Frank Fulsome," writes Mr. Seabury, "flung down the book with disgust and growled an insult at his wife. That little lady put her hands to her face and fled from the room. She was sure Frank must hate her to speak so cruelly. Had she known it, he was not really speaking to her at all. The occasion merely gave vent to a pent-up desire to 'punch his fool boss in the jaw'."

[9]   Max Eastman, *Enjoyment of Laughter* (New York, Simon and Schuster, 1936), p. 343.
[10]   Thurber, *Let Your Mind Alone!* (New York, Harper and Row, 1937). Copr. © 1937 James Thurber; copr. © 1965 Helen W. Thurber and Rosemary Thurber Sauers.

The reader is invited to identify with the simplified stereotypes; the little man can envision himself married to a meek adoring wife, and can dismiss the conflicts within himself by pretending that his motives are as simple and straight-forward as Frank Fulsome's. At the same time the jargon which fills these books may give the reader the notion that he has learned something "scientific". The Frank Fulsome example is supposed to illustrate the concepts of "latent" and "manifest" content of the mind. But of course the concept is meaningless unless part of a much greater context than the "success experts" deal with. Thurber comments,

This "had she known" business is not as common among wives today as Mr. Seabury seems to think it is. The Latent Content (as the psychologists call it) of a husband's mind is usually as clear to the wife as the Manifest Content, frequently much clearer.

Nor does the explanation in any way solve the problem. For whatever reason, Frank has still insulted his wife and "would perhaps be lucky if he didn't get a punch in the jaw himself".

The chaos of experience remains, and no system is adequate to deal with it. When a friend of Thurber's, a man with a Disciplined Mind, encounters a practical joker (also in "Destructive Forces"), the inflexibility of his system leads him to move from his apartment in embarrassment at the loss of dignity he suffers. Thurber concludes:

Hence the undisciplined mind runs far less chance of having its purposes thwarted, its plans distorted, its whole scheme and system wrenched out of line. The undisciplined mind, in short, is far better adapted to the confused world in which we live today than the streamlined mind.

Ultimately, as Thurber says at the beginning, "man will be better off if he quits monkeying with his mind and just lets it alone".

The success experts do not seem to acknowledge that there are problems in the world which no amount of mental discipline can alter. Thurber, of course, is aware that a man with a problem may best begin by trying to account for his own reaction to the situation, and in this endeavor, imagination can be helpful. In

"The Case for the Daydreamer", Thurber confronts Dr. James Mursell, author of *Streamline Your Mind,* a book which favors taking a "definite step to turn your dreams into a reality". The difficulty lies in two notions of what reality is. Thurber tells of being rudely refused a press-pass to a dog-show. In his anger he

wandered up and down the streets of the town, improving on my retorts. I fancied a much more successful encounter with Mr. Bustard. In this fancied encounter, I, in fact, enraged Mr. Bustard. He lunged at me, whereupon, side-stepping agilely, I led with my left and floored him with a beautiful right to the jaw. "Try that one!" I cried aloud. "Mercy!" murmured an old lady who was passing at the moment.

Reality, to Thurber, includes not only the imaginary fight but also the old lady murmuring "mercy!" Obviously this kind of day-dream is no solution; but a better one occurs when Dr. Mursell, the Shaper of Success, is substituted for Thurber:

I fancy that Mr. Bustard also outweighs Dr. Mursell by sixty pounds and is in better fighting trim; we men who write treatises on the mind are not likely to be in as good shape as men who run dog shows. Dr. Mursell, then, is rebuffed, as I was. If he tries to get back at Mr. Bustard right there and then, he will find himself saying "I see" or "Well, I didn't know" or, at best, "I just asked you." Even the streamlined mind runs into this Blockage, as the psychologists call it. Dr. Mursell, like myself, will go away and think up better things to say, but, being a realist dedicated to carrying a dream into actuality, he will perforce have to come back and tackle Mr. Bustard again. If Mr. Bustard's patience gives out, or if he is truly stung by some crack of the Doctor's he is likely to begin shoving, or snap his fingers, or say 'Raus!,' or even tweak the Doctor's nose.

To Thurber, reality must include the ludicrous and the ridiculous — — those aspects of life which drive the little man into fantasy; it is not difficult to make external the "large" injustices which beset man, but the fear of ridicule in small situations is not so easy to — cope with. If a man's car were struck by an irresponsible drunken driver, his anger could be made public with no loss of face; but when Walter Mitty's snow chains become wrapped around the rear axle and a "young, grinning garageman" has to be called, Mitty's humiliation drives him into fantasy: —

The next time, he thought, I'll wear my right arm in a sling; they won't grin at me then. I'll have my right arm in a sling and they'll see I couldn't possibly take the chains off myself.

Daydreams are finally no satisfactory solution either, as Thurber concedes, for as with Mitty, they may lead to loss of identity:

I do not pretend that the daydream cannot be carried too far. If at this late date, for instance, I should get myself up to look as much like Mr. Bustard as possible and then, gazing into the bathroom mirror, snarl "Bustard, you dog!," that would be carrying the day-dream too far. One should never run the risk of identifying oneself with the object of one's scorn.

On the other hand, one's awareness of the fantasy may prevent its becoming destructive.

The technique of the essays in "Let Your Mind Alone!" is quite different from that in *Is Sex Necessary?* In the latter, parody and impersonation combine to provide not only comedy, but a context sufficiently large that the persona could be recognized as a human animal. Thurber's opposition to the success experts is too straightforward for the same effect to be gained. The last two pieces we shall examine here more nearly exhibit the balance of satire and sympathy necessary to successful parody.

In "Something to Say", Thurber's persona tells of a former acquaintance, Elliot Vereker, whose eccentricities were indulged by "Thurber"'s coterie because of the feeling they all had that the man was a genius. "He would have written, but for his philo-sophical indolence, very great novels indeed. We all knew that, and we treated him with a deference for which, now that he is gone, we are sincerely glad." [11] The indignities suffered by Vereker's friends were appalling:

Vereker had a way of flinging himself at a sofa, kicking one end out of it; or he would drop into a fragile chair like a tired bird dog and something would crack. He never seemed to notice. You would invite him to dinner, or, what happened oftener, he would drop in for dinner uninvited, and while you were shaking up a cocktail in the

[11] *The Middle-Aged Man on the Flying Trapeze* (New York, Harper and Row, 1935). Copr. © 1935 James Thurber; copr. © 1963 Helen W. Thurber and Rosemary Thurber Sauers.

kitchen he would disappear. He might go upstairs to wrench the bathtub away from the wall ("breaking lead pipe is one of the truly enchanting adventures in life," he said once). . . .

Vereker's end comes, finally, at a party; he is discovered on the roof, "sprawled on his face, the back of his head crushed in by a blow from some heavy instrument, probably a bottle. He was quite dead. 'The world's loss,' murmured Deane, as he looked down at the pitiful dust so lately the most burning genius we had ever been privileged to know, 'is Hell's gain.' I think we all felt that way."

There is more than mockery in this story of people who indulge psychopaths in the name of genius. The persona emerges as a character capable of being ironic at his own expense, and the irony becomes a means of defending himself against retrospective anger for indignities suffered. The persona is incapable of simply allowing this lunatic to destroy himself:

He frequently threatened suicide and six or seven times attempted it, but in every case, there was someone on hand to prevent him. Once, I remember, he got me out of bed late at night at my apartment. "I'm going through with it this time," he said, and darted into the bathroom. He was fumbling around for some poison in the medicine chest, which fortunately contained none, when I ran in and pleaded with him. "You have so many things yet to do," I said to him. "Yes," he said, "and so many people yet to insult." He talked brilliantly all night long, and drank up a bottle of cognac that I had got to send to my father.

But the narrator recognizes his incapability and asks for neither sympathy nor praise; the irony is always gentle, and it is by this that he seems to remind himself that he *chose* to involve himself in this situation. We lose none of the humor and irony of the tale in recognizing that they enable the narrator to put his dilemma into an enlarged perspective. He is finally capable of genuine admiration for Vereker's indomitable vitality:

We were to make the trip in a huge bus that had been chartered for the purpose. Vereker came along and insisted, when we reached Long Island, on driving the bus. It was an icy night and he would put on the brakes at a curve, causing the heavy vehicle to skid ponderously. Several times we surged perilously near to a ditch and once the bus snapped off a big tree like a match. I remember that H. G. Bennet was along, and Arnold Wells, and the three Sitwells, and four or five Waughs. One of them finally shut off the ignition and another struck Vereker over the head with a crank. His friends were furious. When the car stopped, we carried him outside and put him down on the hard cold ground. Marvin Deane, the critic, held Vereker's head in his lap, looked up at the busload of writers, and said: "You might have killed him! And he is a greater genius than any of you!" It was superb. Then the amazing Vereker opened his eyes. "That goes for me, too," he said, and closed them again.

The combination of an outrageous situation, irony and humanity finally define Thurber's humor. There is enough of Vereker – and certainly of the narrator – in all of us, to warrant an adjustment in our notion of dignity which would allow sufficient flexibility for survival. It is the comic rather than the tragic character who can afford to see himself as sometimes the fool, and it is fools who live long lives.

The price of failing to recognize ourselves as foolish is the subject of one of Thurber's most famous stories, "The Greatest Man in the World".[12] The persona in this tale is, to judge by the style, a journalist of, say, New York *Times* calibre. Perhaps he was even one of those present in the ninth-floor hotel room when Jack "Pal" Smurch was assassinated by order of the President. He aligns himself completely with the forces of order and justice (represented by the politicians, diplomats and newsmen), and implies approval of the murder by his tone of "objectivity". His distaste for the "surly, unprepossessing" juvenile delinquent is evident throughout the story. It is equally evident that the forces of justice, good taste and decency put themselves into a predicament where murder must be committed to preserve the dignity on which justice, good taste and decency rest.

Thurber's scathing attack on the press, which allows itself to be manipulated by politicians, and which in turn manipulates the public, is infinitely more effective than the attack on the Success Experts in *Let Your Mind Alone!*, and in part this results from the impersonation. In his analysis and description of the

---

[12] *Ibid.* Copr. © 1935 James Thurber; copr. © 1963 Helen W. Thurber and Rosemary Thurber Sauers.

Smurch incident, the narrator reveals, by his assumptions, enough about himself to force the reader to see that the main action of the story is centered more nearly about the narrator's response to what he describes, than about Smurch. The narrator is intelligent, sensitive, and well educated – a man of good taste and decency. He appreciates that

> Both Lindbergh and Byrd, fortunately for national decorum and international amity, had been gentlemen; so had our other famous aviators. They wore their laurels gracefully, withstood the awful weather of publicity, married excellent women, usually of fine family, and quietly retired to private life and the enjoyment of their varying fortunes.

But despite the narrator's possession of all the virtues our culture has taught us to admire, he is so dehumanized that he applauds the dehumanization of others. Byrd and Lindbergh were valuable property, but Smurch refuses to accept another identity than his own (the newspapers "arbitrarily" nickname him "Jackie"), and he also refuses to become an instrument for national self-glorification.

The reader of the story – that is, a typical *New Yorker* reader – is put into an extremely awkward position: his every civilized instinct is to identify with the narrator, a man of culture and decency. At the same time, no decent man can believe, as the narrator does, that it was necessary to push Smurch out the window. (International relations survived Lindbergh's embarrassing isolationist statements before World War Two; and more recently, national decorum has been preserved despite Sonny Liston's winning and losing of the heavyweight championship.) The reader is forced to reject the narrator and to recognize that, unlovely as he is, Smurch is a good deal more nearly a human being. We may not wish to identify with Jack Smurch, but we must identify with his hopeless struggle against the whole weight of society to remain himself. Thurber forces us to examine, not so much the power of government and the press, but of our own feelings regarding the basic questions of our Age of Anxiety: Who and what are we?

One of Thurber's central points in "The Greatest Man in the World" is that there is no necessary correlation between the courage required for heroism and the social virtues. The man who can perform the exceptional reminds the rest of us of our shortcomings, and he is acceptable only if he makes other, large concessions to democratic mediocrity; we thus prefer to believe that geniuses are always inept in handling the details of life. Every choice a man makes limits his future choices. One difference between a tragic hero and a comic character is that the former has somehow gone farther along in life before confronting the realization that potential is not unlimited. We have seen in this chapter comic characters who have sought to evade this realization by means of one or another illusion.

But Thurber insists that if we fail to recognize the limitations imposed upon us by life, the result, in our time, is neither nobility nor tragedy but insanity. Thus his comedy becomes a means for accepting reality. He insists upon cutting under the various masquerades which modern man adopts in order to discover the man beneath. Thurber seems to imply that man may not be in such bad shape after all; what is wrong is his illusions but not necessarily his essence – and perhaps something can be done about the former. When illusions become conscious man's position is more nearly hopeful. The individual can more realistically appraise the potential which previously seemed both unlimited and unattainable, and if he has to settle for something less than the mythic dreams, there is no crippling failure in not achieving what is recognized as impossible. But only when one has made this acceptance are fantasies safe. When "Thurber" acknowledges that Mr. Bustard outweighs him by sixty pounds and is in an utterly invulnerable position, then the author can indulge his imagination as a conscious means of ridding himself of anger at the unchangeable. The fantasy is then under control – he can never become a Walter Mitty. Thus is awareness a necessary precursor to acceptance.

III

THURBER'S CLOWN: LIMITATIONS AND ACCEPTANCE

One of comedy's functions is to increase man's awareness of himself and of his world. Such awareness, however, may lead to unpleasant discoveries; knowledge of one's motives, for example, may reveal them as far from noble and heroic. The man whose self-esteem is based on illusions regarding his similarity to cultural stereotypes will almost certainly find it difficult to accept the disillusionment which accompanies awareness. Yet some of Thurber's little men learn to use comedy itself as a means of coming to terms with reality; sometimes they can become self-conscious comedians. Tommy Turner, in *The Male Animal,* solves his dilemma by renouncing dignity and becoming a clown; but, at the end of the play, as we shall later see, Tommy is the most admirable and dignified figure on stage. Comedy, then, is not only a diagnostician's scalpel, but an instrument for acceptance as well.

In the world to be examined here we will notice that Thurber dwells in an area where comedy and pathos come together. There is a clue to the continually shifting relationship between these two elements in a story Thurber told Max Eastman:

My English teacher at Ohio State, Herman A. Miller, told me of something he saw which illustrates [that "People can laugh out of a kind of mellowed self-pity as well as out of superiority"].

One gray and snowy Sunday morning, about 10 o'clock, a smallish husband leading a little fluffy dog on a leash went into a delicatessen store to buy food. Herman said he looked like the cartoon of the Common People in the conventional political caricature. Well, his wife had given him a formidable list of things to buy, so that when he came out of the store both arms were laden with butter, bread, eggs, oranges, etc. It was a problem to handle the dog and the bundles both. Finally, the dog made a lunge and broke away. The man stood there juggling his bundles, dropping one, picking it up, dropping another, calling "Here doggie, here doggie" all the time; then finally setting out onto the icy street, gingerly, in pursuit of the dog. Before he got to it, a car rounded a corner and struck the dog and killed it. The little man just stood there blinking, holding his bundles. That was the highest point of sadness in the scene, all right. But then, still bewildered, always the husband who had to get the groceries home, he tried to pick the dog up and still hold the bundles. After dropping the butter and bread he had to drop the dog again to pick them up. In this amazing moment, there was that almost crazy laugh, for here so closely joined as to be almost incredible, was pathos and slapstick.[1]

The final episode in this situation transforms it from tragedy into tragicomedy; it is Walter Mitty, emerging from fantasy to remember the puppy biscuits, or that his wife likes him to be waiting for her at the hotel. In "The Secret Life of Walter Mitty" the threat of tragedy is implied in the progressive peril of Mitty's fantasies (at the end he stands before the firing squad). The presence of this peril along with absurdity – the "pathos and slapstick" – are central in the work we shall examine here.

The first of these, "The Remarkable Case of Mr. Bruhl" and "The Other Room", have to do with the disappointment implicit in the ever-increasing limitations on life which accompany maturity. Both Mr. Bruhl and Mr. Barrett evince the problems which attend the renunciation of ideals.

Samuel O. Bruhl was just an ordinary-looking citizen, like you and me, except for a curious, shoe-shaped scar on his left cheek which he got when he fell against a wagon-tongue in his youth. He had a good job as treasurer for a syrup-and-fondant concern, a large devout wife, two tractable daughters, and a nice home in Brooklyn. He worked from nine to five, took in a show occasionally, played a bad, complacent game of golf, and was usually in bed by eleven o'clock. The Bruhls had a dog named Bert, a small circle of friends, and an old sedan. They had made a comfortable, if unexciting, adjustment to life.[2]

[1] Quoted in Max Eastman, *Enjoyment of Laughter* (New York, 1936), pp. 342-343.
[2] "The Remarkable Case of Mr. Bruhl", in *The Middle-Aged Man on the Flying Trapeze* (New York, Harper and Row, 1935). Copr. © 1935 James Thurber; copr. © 1963 Helen W. Thurber and Rosemary Thurber Sauers.

Mr. Bruhl, then, is much more nearly the average citizen than Mitty; he is a man who seemingly has accepted the limitations of life without complaint, and is in command of both his job and his home. Yet the story which follows suggests that, because his adjustment has been made, apparently, in a relatively unquestioning fashion, he is even more vulnerable to the perils of uncontrolled fantasy than Mitty.

It happens that Bruhl bears a resemblance to a notorious gangster, George ("Shoescar") Clinigan. In the course of New York gang wars, Clinigan is wounded and his pictures appear in the papers; Bruhl's business associates remark upon the resemblance. Mr. Bruhl becomes increasingly upset as the papers print reports that rival gangsters are after "Shoescar"; a practical joker at the office makes threatening phone calls to Mr. Bruhl. Though the joke is exposed, Mr. Bruhl begins acting more and more strangely, "skulking about, starting at every noise, and once almost fainting when an automobile backfired near him".

Samuel Bruhl began to take on a remarkable new appearance. He talked out of the corner of his mouth, his eyes grew shifty. He looked more and more like Shoescar Clinigan. He snarled at his wife. Once he called her "Babe," and he had never called her anything but Minnie. He kissed her in a strange, new way, acting rough, almost brutal.

Clearly, the male animal is beginning to emerge; Bruhl now keeps a revolver under his pillow, and once he takes a shot at the mantel clock, hitting it "squarely in the middle". He stops going to work and lounges around the house in his pajamas, smoking cigarettes and reading books about other famous gangsters.

The doctor who finally came and slipped into Bruhl's bedroom was very grave when he emerged. "This is a psychosis," he said, "a definite psychosis. Your husband is living in a world of fantasy. He has built up a curious defense mechanism against something or other."

Instead of getting a psychiatrist, as the doctor urged, Mrs. Bruhl takes her husband on a trip out of town. At a little inn in the mountains, Mr. Bruhl is resting, but his delusion has in no way abated. Four men enter the empty dining room of the inn where

Bruhl is playing the mechanical piano, take guns from their music cases, and shoot Mr. Bruhl. As he is dying, Mrs. Bruhl and the Police Commissioner try to get him to describe his assassins.

"I don't know what they looked like," snarled Bruhl, "and if I did know I wouldn't tell you." He was silent a moment, then: "Cop!" he added bitterly. The Commissioner sighed and turned away. "They're all like that," he said to the others in the room. "They never talk." Hearing this, Mr. Bruhl smiled, a pleased smile, and closed his eyes.

The ending confirms what the reader has suspected all along – that Bruhl delights, unconsciously, in this role so dissimilar to his real self. Apparently, the "something or other" against which he has built up this "curious defense mechanism" is the comfortable and unexciting adjustment he has made to life, an adjustment which renounced the dreams all of us have of fame and fortune. In middleage, Mr. Bruhl is offered what seems to be a substitute for the choice made earlier, and he takes it. But, of course, one cannot change his identity any more than he can alter the fact of having made previous choices.

Mr. Barrett, in "The Other Room", has also made a "normal" adjustment to life, but at more evident cost than Mr. Bruhl's. Barrett, however, emerges at the end in a far stronger position. "Thurber" and his wife sit in the bar of the Hotel Continental in Paris waiting for three persons: a twenty-two-year-old American girl, and the Barretts, friends of friends who were supposed to be looked-up. Meanwhile, they meet a painter friend. When Linda, the girl, arrives, she tells the others of an adventure she has just had, "not a very pleasant one". A middle-aged American has tried to pick her up:

"He said '*Combien pour toute la nuit?*' " she said.

"He *must* be at least sixty," I said. "That goes back to the battle of Paris in the First World War. I know all the verses."[3]

Linda goes on –

"I just looked at him," Linda said, "and told him, 'I am an American girl.' I really put my best Sunday virtue into it. Funny, he seemed to

---

[3]   Thurber, *Credos and Curios* (New York, Harper and Row, 1962). Copr. © 1962 Helen W. Thurber.

look at me and past me too. It was odd, and gave me the shivers a little. Then he said something I didn't understand and walked away."

Soon this same man comes into the bar and, inevitably, is Mr. Barrett. The narrator greets him, " 'You been behaving yourself, Mr. Barrett?' "

"Have to," he said. "Got the little woman with me, you know." We managed the introduction somehow. Barrett recognized Linda, there was no doubt about that. He was for three seconds a statue in bronze, a frightened statue, a little tired, a little older than the man who had walked into the room.

Barrett's wife, he tells them, is resting in the hotel. Barrett breaks the awkward silence by telling of an adventure of his own. Forty years before, he had been in Paris following the battle of Fère-en-Tardenois. He had been wounded and hospitalized and had escaped from the hospital to Paris, where he had met a young prostitute. They had shared their loneliness walking around for a while and then had gone to her room.

... there were pictures of guys all over her living room, guys in uniform, guys of all the allied countries. The picture I can't forget was a picture of a young Canadian soldier. . . . He was a handsome fella, and he couldn't have been more than twenty himself."

He interrupts his story to tell that the Canadian soldier – who had been killed – and sometimes the girl, continually appear in his dreams. The girl, he continues, goes into the other room and Barrett sits looking at the pictures and thinking of his girl at home in Iowa, now his wife. The girl calls to him from the other room and Barrett is forced to renounce the romantic illusions he has constructed about her; she is, after all, still a prostitute. Suddenly he is frightened and flees to the street, still carrying his glass of wine.

"I put it down somewhere, and went on walking. I must've walked for miles. The next thing I really remember I was back at the hospital. I guess the MPs got me. . . . After that, for a while, I went into a nose dive, kinda what the docs call nervous prostitution."

(His slip is allowed to go unnoticed.) In the dreams, the door to the other room "is always locked, or something, or the floor to the other room is gone, like it was blown away". After the story Barrett gets up to leave.

Linda suddenly stood up, and ran, rather than walked, around the table. She was tall . . . almost as tall as Barrett, so she did not have to stand on tiptoe when she kissed him on the forehead. "I like you," she said, warmly. "I think you're lovely." He patted her hand twice, and then said something none of us could understand, and hurriedly walked away.

The story ends with the narrator singing *"Combien pour toute la nuit?"* to the others in a cab.

"The Other Room" brings together a number of clichés, and in so doing achieves a statement, at the end, quite beyond the power of any clichés. The middle-aged vulgar American tourist, come to Paris for a last fling – while his wife rests in the hotel – is juxtaposed with the boy who has come across the sea to fight a glorious war to discover that war is hell; but Thurber has filled out the clichés with details which lift Barrett above the stereotype. Furthermore, the envelope in which Barrett's tale is enclosed serves to forestall stockresponses in the reader to the clichés of the situation; these responses, suggested or acted out by the narrator and his companions, are submitted to the reader as further evidence in the case of Mr. Barrett. The boy, Barrett, was filled with the hopes we all have for the unlimited potential of life. But maturity for him has been realized in terms of ever-increasing limitations. Death itself, as symbolized in his dreams by the Canadian soldier, is one of these, and the realization that the girl was still only a prostitute is another. Barrett's ability to tell this unflattering story on himself implies some measure of acceptance of himself and his life – an acceptance which brings together slapstick and pathos. We need feel little pity for Barrett since he has at least partly purged himself of pity.

But if we do not pity Barrett, neither do we admire him. One sees his life as a series of defenses; there is just enough suppleness in the man for him to bounce back after each blow. But there is none of the aggressiveness which enables one to meet life head-on and to enjoy its conflicts: this requires either a clown or a hero.

The kind of suppleness that makes for a clown is a major,

though an unwitting, part of Mr. Martin, the little man in "The Catbird Seat".[4] Martin is head of the filing department of F & S, and his position there is threatened by Mrs. Ulgine Barrows, "the newly appointed special advisor to the president of the firm, Mr. Fitweiler". Martin is perfectly aware of the role he plays at F & S: a dry, meticulous little man. The role, as we shall see, is necessary to contain the turmoil within him. Martin is always conscious that Mr. Fitweiler had once said, "Man is fallible but Martin isn't." So well established is his masquerade as the essence of Milquetoast that he can depend upon it to commit his crime. He conceives of a "casual and bold" plan to "rub out" the "obstacle", Mrs. Barrows, who not only threatens his position with F & S, but offends him daily with her braying laugh and her baseball idioms, borrowed from Red Barber: Are you lifting the oxcart out of the ditch? Are you tearing up the pea patch? Are you hollering down the rain barrel? Are you scraping around the bottom of the pickle barrel? Are you sitting in the catbird seat?

The abstemious Martin plans to go to her apartment, smoke cigarettes and drink whiskey, and then murder the woman with a weapon which he expects to find in her room; the plan is perfect, for no one will connect this bold crime with the mild little filing department supervisor. But the plan is too much for Martin; confronted with the actual woman, who is much larger than he, his courage leaves him before he can decide upon a murder weapon. Inspiration comes at the last minute. She has seen him smoking and drinking already; all he has to do is enhance this second masquerade:

"Here's nuts to that old windbag, Fitweiler," he said, and gulped again. The stuff tasted awful, but he made no grimace. "Really, Mr. Martin," she said, her voice and posture changing, "you are insulting our employer." Mrs. Barrows was now all special adviser to the president. "I am preparing a bomb," said Mr. Martin, "which will blow the old goat higher than hell." He had only had a little of the drink, which was not strong. It couldn't be that. "Do you take dope

---

[4] *The Thurber Carnival* (New York, Harper and Row, 1945). Copr. © 1945 James Thurber.

or something?" Mrs. Barrows asked coldly. "Heroin," said Mr. Martin. "I'll be coked to the gills when I bump that old buzzard off."

Next morning, Mrs. Barrows sweeps into Mr. Fitweiler's office, and soon Martin is called for.

Mr. Fitweiler was pale and nervous. He took his glasses off and twiddled them. He made a small, bruffing sound in his throat. "Martin," he said, "you have been with us more than twenty years." "Twenty-two, sir," said Mr. Martin. "In that time," pursued the president, "your work and your – uh – manner have been exemplary." "I trust so, sir," said Mr. Martin. "I have understood, Martin," said Mr. Fitweiler, "that you have never taken a drink or smoked." "That is correct, sir," said Mr. Martin. "Ah, yes." Mr. Fitweiler polished his glasses. "You may describe what you did after leaving the office yesterday, Martin," he said. Mr. Martin allowed less than a second for his bewildered pause. . . .

In a moment Martin is informed of Mrs. Barrows' "delusion". " 'It is the nature of these psychological diseases,' Mr. Fitweiler said, 'to fix upon the least likely and most innocent party as the – uh – source of persecution. . . . I am afraid Mrs. Barrows' usefulness here is at an end.' " Mrs. Barrows is carried out of the office, screaming imprecations at the bewildered Martin. Mr. Fitweiler apologizes to Martin, who returns to his office "wearing a look of studious concentration".

In *The Years with Ross,* Thurber describes a little man who may have suggested the character of Martin to him; by comparing the portrait of Harold Winney in *Ross,* to that of Mr. Martin, we can see how this fictional little man preserved himself as Harold Winney could not. Winney was Ross's secretary from 1935 until August, 1941. Thurber describes his "cold small voice, his pale nimble fingers, and his way of moving about the corridors and offices like a shadow". In his tenure with Ross, Winney managed to embezzle seventy-one thousand dollars from his employer, most of which he apparently spent on his men friends and at the race tracks. When he would have been caught he committed suicide. The comparison is interesting, for it makes explicit the violent contrast in the outward and inner nature of both of these men. The other Martin is revealed in the fantasy of killing Mrs. Barrows, but, unlike Winney, Martin is able to contain his less acceptable self within a disguise. Martin is put into a comic situation in which it is possible for him to acknowledge his masquerade by his improbable burlesque of an opposite role with Mrs. Barrows. "The Secret Life of Harold Winney" is a study in the grotesque; the story of Mr. Martin is comedy, for in it the pathetic, the slapstick, and the grotesque merge to make a statement which is more important than the mere fact that beneath every Milquetoast beats the heart of a criminal.

Clowns, in some respects, are privileged persons in our society. The self-conscious comedian is allowed to show his anger at anomalies in our culture or at individuals in ways that the man concerned to preserve his dignity cannot afford. In "File and Forget", the Thurber persona wears the clown's mask to suggest the masks businessmen employ to shield themselves from other people. The piece implies that one can avoid the businessman's uniformity only if he exaggerates his own eccentricities.

"File and Forget" is a series of exasperating letters between "Thurber" and a publisher who mistakenly assumes that "Thurber" has ordered thirty-six copies of a book called *Grandma Was a Nudist*. The tone is established by a prefatory statement:

I want to thank my secretary, Miss Ellen Bagley, for putting the following letters in order. I was not up to the task myself, for reasons that will, I think, become clear to the reader.[5]

The letters which follow expose every odious social aspect of the modern business world, as well as the reaction of the little man to them. The first letter replies to the publisher's acknowledgment of the supposed order, which has been missent to several of Thurber's former addresses; Thurber begins by trying to straighten out the mistaken address:

Your company, in the great tradition of publishers, has sent so many letters to me at Hot Springs, Ark., that the postmaster there has simply taken to sending them on to the right address, or what would be the right address if I were there. . . . Another publishing firm recently sent a letter to me at 65 West 11th Street, an address I vacated in the summer of 1930. It would not come as a surprise to me if your

[5] *Thurber Country* (New York, Simon and Schuster, 1953). Copr. ©
1953 James Thurber.

firm or some other publishers, wrote me in care of my mother at 568 Oak street, Columbus, Ohio. I was thirteen years old when we lived there, back in 1908.

He goes on to explain that he did not order *Grandma Was a Nudist* and does not want the books. Meanwhile the books are delivered to another address, vacated in 1944, and Thurber sends the Post Office notice to the publisher with another letter from which all the chattiness of the first letter is missing. The only acknowledgment of his denial of ordering *Grandma Was a Nudist* is the postscript appended to one of the letters: "P.S. What you had to say about 'Grandma' amused us all." The assumption implicit in the tone of Thurber's first letter – that the secretary was capable of joining him in irony at the expense of the Organization – is answered in her postscripted response. Clearly such frivolity can be tolerated only in a humorist – for whom a stock response awaits.

Pratfall follows pratfall as the books are, inevitably, shipped to the Columbus address. When the shipping department discovers who it was that really ordered *Grandma*, they assume that what Thurber wanted was thirty-six copies of one of his own books. In desperation, Thurber writes the president of the firm (who is in California on business) and then to an old friend, ending this letter: "I don't want any more copies of my book. I don't want any more copies of my book. I don't want any more copies of my book." Unfortunately he has signed this letter "Jim" and unfortunately his friend is no longer with the firm. In reply he receives a letter from his friend's successor, addressed: "Dear Jim Thurber." What follows is a fine collection of businessman jargon.

I haven't had the pleasure of meeting you since I had the great good luck to join forces with Charteriss, but I look forward to our meeting with a high heart. . . . I should like to wine and dine you and perhaps discuss the new book that I feel confident you have in you. If you don't want to talk shop, we can discuss the record of our mutual football team. You were at Northwestern some years ahead of my time, I believe, but I want you to know that they still talk about Jimmy Thurber out there [in "University Days" Thurber wrote of his life and hard times at Ohio State]. . . . I want you to feel, however, that every single one of us here is your friend, willing and eager to do your slightest bidding. All of us feel very deeply about your having turned against your book "Thurber's Ark." . . . Well, Jim, let me assure you that this is just a passing fancy. . . . I am banking on twenty years' experience in the book publishing game when I take the liberty of sending these twenty books off to you today.

The blunders continue: *Grandma* catches up with Thurber again, and someone else at Charteriss asks for information, but has no recollection of having asked when the information comes. Thurber's secretary then writes a note informing the publisher that "Mr. Thurber has had one of his spells as a result of the multiplication of books and misunderstanding. . . . He proposes to burn all 72 books in the middle of U.S. Highway No. 7." Finally, "Mr. Thurber wishes me to tell you that he does not want to hear from any of you again." More letters follow and the piece concludes with a letter from Thurber's mother which begins, "I don't understand the clipping from the Lakeville *Journal* Helen's mother [Thurber's mother-in-law] sent me, about someone burning all those books of yours in the street." Outrage and absurdity are combined here to make "File and Forget" one of Thurber's most painfully funny pieces, but some of the sense of outrage is released in Thurber's outrageous burning of the books, and further, by his exposure of the whole situation by means of this story.

The reader of "File and Forget" can empathize with the little man's plight and with his anger, but he also recognizes that "Thurber" the satirist has repaid the score by the very means of exposing his own discomfiture. Sometimes the undignified, undisciplined man is more capable of meeting the chaos of our world than the man dominated by preconceived notions of right behavior and wrong. Perhaps the best example of this is Tommy Turner in *The Male Animal*; however, discussion of this play will be postponed until after brief reviews of two other stories, "Everything is Wild" and "The Ordeal of Mr. Matthews".

Mr. and Mrs. Brush, in "Everything is Wild", have been invited to a dinner party by acquaintances in the suburbs, and Mr. Brush is displeased about it. He won't be able to find their hosts' apartment, he fears; there will be a lot of awful guests; and people will talk of nothing but business and baseball. The Brushes, as it happens, are the only guests, and dinner and conversation are pleasant. But after dinner another couple drops in and they decide to play poker – not good old man-style straight poker, but effeminate variations like Duck-in-the-Pond, Seven-Card Stud (with deuces and treys wild), and Poison Ivy. Mr. Brush suffers in grouchy silence until the deal comes to him, at which point he invents a wild game of his own which he calls Soap-in-Your-Eye ("Out West they call it Kick-in-the-Pants"). The game is hopelessly complex and Mr. Brush wins the hand more or less by default. Shortly thereafter the Brushes leave:

... in silence they drove off. Mr. Brush at last began to chortle. "Darn good game, Soap-in-Your-Eye," he said. Mrs. Brush stared at him, evilly, for a full minute. "You terrible person," she said. Mr. Brush broke into loud and hearty laughter. He ho-hoed all the way down the Grand Concourse. He had had a swell time after all.[6]

Mr. Brush has successfully resisted the threats to his dominance of social situations. But the price for his dominance, one suspects, is a continuing war with his wife; his weapon is the anger which he threatens to brandish at anyone who gets in his way, and his mockery of the other poker players, though it is funny, makes no effort to conceal the contempt he feels for them. But it is important that we distinguish between the use to which Brush puts his anger, and the use of anger in "File and Forget". The title is a clue in the latter. Once the issue has been revealed, it can be forgotten. But Mr. Brush discovers nothing through his little charade; instead he has confirmed his prejudice, and the charade disguises the realities of the situation, and can only provide further material for his contempt of people. Like Mitty and Bruhl, Brush can only further isolate himself.

In "The Ordeal of Mr. Matthews", as in so many of Thurber's cocktail-party conversations, the narrator poses as a little man, a comic figure who can afford to seem almost, indeed, the fool. The piece can almost be taken as an allegory concerning modern

---

[6] *The Middle-Aged Man on the Flying Trapeze.* Copr. © 1935 James Thurber; copr. © 1963 Helen W. Thurber and Rosemary Thurber Sauers.

humor and its audience. At a party in the country, Thurber traps a businessman named Matthews and begins lecturing on his favorite subject: Humor, its decline and its usefulness. He begins by quoting famous wits of the past – Joseph Choate, Disraeli, Swope – and then begins listing witty things he has been quoted as saying. As a counterpoint to Thurber's monologue, Matthews makes brief if irrelevant comments. Thurber repeats Wilkes' famous retort to Sandwich (" 'That depends, sir, on whether I embrace your mistress or your principles' "), and Matthews remarks: "Had 'em more openly in those days, of course – mistresses." When, at the end, Matthews has finally had enough, Thurber comments, "He had pretty well worn me out." [7]

No form of communication, it would seem, can connect the intellectual and the businessman, not even humor. But upon closer examination, perhaps it isn't so. After all, there is an audience which will read about Mr. Matthews and perhaps see something of itself in the mirror. Thurber tells Matthews of his own witticisms which have been publicly quoted, and the piece does not end with Matthews walking away. Another guest tells Thurber,

"John Matthews has been telling us a perfectly wonderful story, Mr. Thurber," she squealed, "about how you absolutely refused to rewrite 'Alice in Wonderland,' in spite of all the money they offered you."

Matthews has gotten it all wrong, of course; Thurber had been asked to do illustrations for a new edition and had replied, "Let's keep the Tenniel drawings and I'll rewrite the story." Nevertheless, Matthews was trying. And Thurber himself keeps on trying. As they leave, his wife asks him why he was shouting at one of the lady guests:

"Madam," I said, "if a man shouts at Ida Barlow, he makes an ass of her, but if he does not shout at Ida Barlow, he makes an ass of himself. . . . Ask me why I didn't fall off the wagon?"
   She sighed. "All right, why didn't you fall off the wagon?"
   "They didn't have any formaldehyde," I chortled. It didn't strike

[7]   Thurber, *The Beast in Me and Other Animals* (New York, Harcourt, Brace and World, 1948). Copr. © 1948 James Thurber.

her as funny, for some reason, but I had to laugh. I laughed most of the way home.

The ending to this piece is almost identical to the ending of "Everything is Wild" – that is, the words are nearly the same. But Thurber has alienated no one at the party, and *contempt* would certainly not describe his attitude toward the other guests. Thurber turns anger into comedy which lacks the vindictiveness of Mr. Brush's mockery. The Thurber persona achieves a balance between the parts of him which set him off from the community and those he shares with the rest of society.

The difference between these two types of character can perhaps be seen most clearly if we examine some of the figures in *The Male Animal*.[8] Ed Keller, principal tyrant and Red-hater on the board of trustees, is similar to Mr. Brush in his almost childish demands for the things he wants. Joe Ferguson reminds us of Mr. Matthews; unimaginative and insensitive, he has made a comfortable adjustment to life, and fully believes in the things he is supposed to believe in. At first, Tommy Turner seems an unlikely person to oppose such forceful men as these. A young associate professor of English at a large mid-western university, which has just undergone a red-purge, Tommy seems the last man to involve himself in a conflict which can only lead to his defeat. Yet circumstances force the role of hero upon him.

A student of Tommy's, who is editor of the literary magazine, publishes a scathing denunciation of the trustees who had fired three professors for supposed communist affiliations, and announces that there is one faculty member left who has not been cowed. Professor Turner, the editorial continues, dares to teach "what he believes should be taught. . . . He is not afraid to bring

---

[8]   Copr. © 1940 (Acting Edition). James Thurber and Elliott Nugent (New York, Samuel French, Inc., 1940). Mrs. Helen Thurber, in a letter, provided the following information regarding the collaboration between Thurber and Elliott Nugent: "Thurber's plot concerned only the 3 main characters originally. Nugent added the Vanzetti theme, and wrote the entire scene of the reading of the letter. Thurber, as is evident, wrote all the dialogue for the party scene in Act I, the drunk scene in 2nd Act, the final scene. Most of the others were collaborative."

up even the Sacco-Vanzetti case. He has read to his classes on the same day Vanzetti's last statement and Lincoln's letter to Mrs. Bixby." Tommy has not actually read the letters, but he had mentioned to Michael, the editor, that he intended to do so. All this while, Tommy's household is in turmoil in anticipation of guests; it is homecoming weekend and there is to be a dinner for Joe Ferguson, ex-football hero and ex-boy-friend of Ellen Turner. Keller is an old friend of Joe's, and has thus been invited, and Tommy is unhappy about this. Dean Damon, head of the English Department, has come earlier to warn Tommy about Michael's editorial; they agree to keep the matter from Keller, but during the party, Mrs. Damon (sorely afflicted with the foot-in-mouth disease) lets the affair out, and Keller threatens Tommy: "Turner, you better think twice before you read anything. I can promise you the trustees will clamp down on any professor who tries anything funny." He is furious about Michael's editorial and promises to have the boy expelled – which he later succeeds in doing. At the threat, Tommy begins to think more seriously about reading the letter, and Ellen is upset with him for jeopardizing his career.

Joe, we learn, is divorcing his wife, and Ellen turns to him in her anger at Tommy. Tommy is supposed to be upstairs at one point, but he comes down in time to see Joe and Ellen dancing closely. Tommy and Ellen become more and more distant. Tommy can't seem to make her understand how he feels about submitting to Keller's threat, and as he feels himself losing her to Joe, he announces that he is leaving her and insists that Joe take her away. In a parallel sub-plot, Michael, who has been competing with a football player, Wally Myers, for Ellen's sister, Patricia, finds himself rejected by Pat because of the editorial. Tommy and Michael get drunk together and as the male animal in them emerges, they recognize their own ineffectuality; when Joe comes in, Tommy picks a fight with him and Joe, reluctantly, beats him up.

A storm of publicity arises over Michael's editorial and Tommy is confronted with the realization that he has lost both his job and wife. Keller, Joe, and Damon come, and Keller once again threatens Tommy. Tommy angrily denounces Keller and implies his contempt for Dean Damon who has refused to take a stand on the academic freedom issue. He reads them the letter, which is politically harmless, and this deflates the issue – except to Keller, whose motives are far from rational: "If he reads this letter to his class he'll get a lot of those kids worried about that man. Make socialists out of 'em." Tommy's anger arouses even the complacent Dean Damon:

Mr. Keller, for forty-two years I have followed a policy of appeasement ... there is an increasing element in the faculty which resents your attitude toward any teacher who raises his voice or so much as clears his throat. I warn you that if you persist in persecuting Thomas Turner, you will have a fight on your hands, my friend. (Act 3.)

Tommy has also succeeded in arousing Ellen, but when she tenders sympathy he rejects it and repeats his insistence that she go away with Joe. (By this time Joe is thoroughly frightened that she may indeed do this. What, after all, would his little Presbyterian suburb think of him, divorcing one wife and bringing home someone else's!) At the end, Joe soothes over all wounded feelings, and Tommy and Ellen are dancing together before Tommy goes to class to read the letter.

Simply from the plot we can get a fair idea of the major characters in this play. As always in Thurber, there is a curious mixture of dependence upon and independence from stereotypes. Tommy seems, at first, a Milquetoast in the tradition of Mitty: emotionally dependent upon his wife, academically cloistered, a trifle absent-minded, a "pussy-cat". But the details by which his character is realized give him another dimension. Tommy is conscious, as no stereotype can be, of the roles he plays, and throughout the play this awareness is revealed in remarks which show him to be a self-conscious clown, using wit to keep in touch with reality. Before the party Damon is concerned with pacifying Ed Keller. "Since he must be with us tonight let us confine our conversation to the – woeful inadequacies of the Illinois team." Tommy gently reminds him that the game is with Michigan – and we realize that Tommy is not so cloistered as Damon. When

Tommy and Ellen reminisce about Joe's interfering with their dates, Tommy pretends immense ignorance about football:

Remember how Joe was always horning in on our dinner dates? I don't believe we ever had one that he didn't come over and diagram the Washington Monument play or something on the tablecloth with a pencil. (Act 1.)

This time it is Ellen who points out to the absent-minded professor that he means the Statue of Liberty play. But later, when Joe is demonstrating the play to Ellen and Pat with a teacup, Tommy sneaks in behind him, takes the cup from his hand and disappears through a French door before Joe realizes what has happened. (Joe never discovers how the cup disappeared.) Again, during the party while Keller, Joe, and the others babble on about the game, Tommy quietly sings "Who's afraid of the big red team", reducing the whole affair to the level of a nursery rhyme and infuriating Keller. At the end, Keller, who is shocked at the idea of Joe running off with Ellen, tells Joe his worst fear: "Why – they'll never ask us to the Rose Bowl now!" Tommy asks blandly, "What is the Rose Bowl?"

Similarly, Tommy's absent-mindedness seems part of a comic act. Ellen accuses Tommy, in the opening scene, of having stolen the matchboxes she had placed in ash trays.

TOMMY. *(Digging in his pockets).* I haven't seen any match-boxes. *(She finds two. He smiles guiltily.)* Say, you look very pretty tonight. That's a new dress, isn't it?
ELLEN.   ... No. ... One more [match box].
TOMMY. Oh, you exaggerate this match-box thing. Oh! *(Hands her one. . .).*

As in the conversation about the "Washington Monument play" one senses that Tommy plays this role because it seems to be what Ellen expects of him, and when they argue, we get an idea why. A recurring motif in their arguments is Ellen's intellectual insecurity.

ELLEN.   ... Tommy, you're not going to go ahead and read that letter.
TOMMY. Yes, Ellen, I think I have to.

ELLEN.   Tommy, try to be practical for once. At least wait until you're not so mad. Try to think of this the way any other man would think of it.

TOMMY.   I'm not any other man.... I don't see why you don't try to understand how *I* feel about this....

ELLEN.   Oh, you and your mind! I have to go through such a lot with your mind.... Oh, I know, I know! I'm too dumb for you. (Act 1.)

As a way of balancing their relationship, Tommy plays at being impractical and absent-minded, and thus does not threaten Ellen's control over her home. Yet there is no evidence that he is actually impractical. Even his insistence upon reading the letter is based partly on his knowledge that other teachers have been dismissed for no real cause and that Keller's dominance of academic affairs is intolerable. Acquiescence to Keller offers him no security for it sets a precedent which can only work against him. The actual importance of the academic freedom issue is integral to the play's structure, for without freedom, Tommy's profession will be far less attractive. He makes the most practical decision, for he stands to lose nothing and there is the possibility of gaining a great deal. He is fully aware that there is no chance of persuading Keller; but he may – and he does – awaken Damon and also makes Ellen and Joe aware of the situation's actual nature.

Also, his handling of the threat Joe seems to pose to his marriage is essentially practical. He sees that the real issue is between Ellen and himself. It is not a matter of making a concession to Ellen, to convince her that he is "practical" the way she thinks Joe is. They can continue together only with an enlarged knowledge of themselves and each other. Tommy has played the clown before, as we have seen, in order to ingratiate himself with Ellen; now he plays the fool in order to establish his identity.

When he learned, early in the play, that Joe's marriage had broken up, he expressed sympathy.

JOE.   No, it's all fine. We're both taking it in our stride. Took her out to dinner last week – along with her new boy friend....

TOMMY.   Wasn't that rather complicated?

ELLEN.   Oh, you're not up to date, Tommy. That's the modern way
          of doing things. (Act 1.)

Later Tommy parodies the absurdity of this "modern way", can-
didly telling Joe the things he must do to keep Ellen happy, until
Joe complains, "This is embarrassing! . . . A man makes love to
a woman. He doesn't talk it over with her husband!" Tommy
replies: "I'm just trying to be honest." Tommy continues to peel
away the layers of illusion which disguise the situation, urging
Joe to go upstairs to comfort Ellen.

JOE.   Oh, no. Not me! You ought to know what to do right now.
          It's your house. She's still your wife.
TOMMY.   . . . She doesn't want to talk to me. She's just done that. But
          she oughtn't to be left alone right now. (*Joe hesitates.*) Well,
          don't be a big baby!!
JOE.   . . . It doesn't seem right somehow for me to go upstairs.
TOMMY.   This is not a moment for cheap moralizing. (Act 2, Scene 1.)

Again, Tommy tries on the bourgeois morality he despises by
means of parody. He tells Michael:

If the male animal in you doesn't like the full implication of being
civilized, he must nevertheless be swayed by Reason. You are not
living in the days of King Arthur when you fought for your woman.
. . . Nowadays, the man and his wife and the other man talk it over.
Quietly and calmly. They all go out to dinner together.

(Act 2, Scene 1.)

He and Michael then get drunk together:

TOMMY.   Let us say that the tiger wakes up one morning and finds
          that the wolf has come down on the fold. What does he –?
          Before I tell you what he does, I will tell you what he does
          not do. . . . He does not expose everyone to a humiliating
          intellectual analysis. He comes out of his corner like
          this –. . . . The bull elephant in him is aroused. . . . The sea
          lion knows better. He snarls. He gores. He roars with his
          antlers. He knows that love is a thing you do something
          about. He knows that love is a thing that words can kill.
          (Act 2, Scene 2.)

Tommy is both consciously mocking the football players who
threaten both him and Michael, and at the same time is trying

on their role; it is necessary for him to actually fight Joe – which he does shortly after the "male animal" monologue – for him to prove to himself it is no more satisfactory than his own role.

In the end, Tommy uses the "intellectual analysis" the tiger deplores to establish certain realities. For example it is useful in encouraging Ellen's self-esteem, and in goading Joe. Ellen and Tommy are throwing things and Joe intervenes:

JOE.   *(Leaps for Tommy – grabs saucer from him.)* Now wait – let me handle this. I don't throw things – I just want to say that I came to this city to see a football game.

ELLEN.   . . . Oh, no, you didn't! You came for me. You haven't been here for a ball-game in ten years. You wait till Brenda and you are separated, then you come for me!

JOE.   Oh, hell! *(Throws saucer in fireplace, then wilts as he realizes this household has affected him, too.)*

TOMMY.   . . . That's very smart, Ellen. That's very penetrating. That's all I wanted to know. *(To Joe.)* Subconsciously, you came here for Ellen, so don't try to deny it.

JOE.   . . . I don't do things subconsciously! You're full of childish explanations of everything that comes up!

TOMMY.   And you're full of psychological evasions!

ELLEN.   *(Screaming.)* Oh, shut up! Both of you! I am not going to listen to any more of this! *(Runs upstairs.)* (Act 3.)

They are, as Tommy demonstrates, civilized people, but recognizing this does not decrease the importance of emotions any more than fighting is a satisfactory release for them. Ellen sees Tommy in command of this situation and flees from her sudden awareness that her symbolic conception of her husband is false; Tommy is far more realistic – which is to say, practical – than Joe. It is only after Ellen recognizes this that Tommy can afford to take her back.

The battle between little men and the world's practical people is joined in this play, and in Tommy we have a Thurber little man who can come to terms with life. Unlike Mitty, Tommy's consciousness of his masquerades prevents their becoming a destructive force in his life. Unlike Mr. Brush – and Ed Keller – Tommy has no strong feeling that he must protect his dignity or his masquerade. But ironically, Tommy emerges at the end of the play with more dignity than anyone else, for only he – and to a limited extent, Ellen – is truly aware of the forces which motivate people. In a chaotic world where issues are not clear, it can sometimes be more valuable to understand the complexities and to insist upon the suspension of judgment. Tommy stands to lose less, even if Keller can get him fired, than Keller will if the faculty successfully revolts against his domination. Keller's identity is too closely – and too subconsciously – bound to his tyranny over the board of trustees for him not to suffer greatly if this is shattered. Tommy has no such vulnerability, and this is where his strength lies.

IV

AN EDUCATION FOR HARD TIMES

In a sense, Thurber's "autobiographical" stories resemble the "education" books so abundant in American literature. Like Franklin's *Autobiography, Huckleberry Finn,* and Henry Adams' *Education, My Life and Hard Times* records the experiences of a young man, his adventures at home and his first journeys into the world. Thurber's education perhaps prepared him more successfully than any of the others'; it taught him to become a self-conscious clown, to use comedy to balance himself in a chaotic world. The organization of these stories typically reflects this education; at first it may seem that there is no order – one of the narrator's recollections leads to another, with little apparent method. But eventually, we realize that the narration really involves a double imposture, and from this a pattern emerges. At one moment, the narrator is a child, reliving the incident; at another, he is a man, looking backwards, and attempting to reconcile his youthful memories and impressions with mature knowledge and judgment. In the best of these stories, the isolation and alienation which seem to pervade American literature are overcome.

In order to see how this isolation is overcome, let us look first at two stories in which it is a major element. "One is a Wanderer" is not explicitly "autobiographical" like "The Luck of Jad Peters"; however, it was written shortly after Thurber's first marriage ended, and it is not difficult to see the author's identification with the protagonist, Kirk. This man wanders slowly along Fifth Avenue, postponing the return to "home":

It would be gloomy and close in his hotel room, and his soiled shirts would be piled on the floor of the closet where he had been flinging them for weeks, where he had been flinging them for months, and his papers would be disarranged on the tops of the tables and on the desk, and his pipes would be lying around, the pipes he had smoked determinedly for a while only to give them up, as he always did, to go back to cigarettes. He turned into the street leading to his hotel, walking slowly, trying to decide what to do with the night. He had had too many nights alone. Once he had enjoyed being alone. Now it was hard to be alone. He couldn't read anymore, or write, at night. Books he tossed aside after nervously flipping through them; the writing he tried to do turned into spirals and circles and squares and empty faces.[1]

The last image reminds us of Kinstrey, whose whip-poor-will rolled "its loops and circles of sound" into his dreams. Kirk's fantasies will never dominate him as Kinstrey's did, but where the latter's outward life was well-ordered, Kirk's is chaotic. Kirk wanders about for a while, considers going to a movie ("the kind of movie that didn't bother you") but reflects that he has already been to one film that day.

He goes back to the hotel, has several brandies, and considers visiting people who had been friends before:

He saw the Graysons, not as they would be, sitting in their apartment, close together and warmly, but as he and Lydia had seen them in another place and another year. The four had shared a bright vacation once. He remembered various attitudes and angles and lights and colors of that vacation. There is something about four people, two couples, that like each other and get along; that have a swell time; that grow in intimacy and understanding. One's life is made up of twos, and of fours. The Graysons understood the nice little arrangements of living, the twos and fours. Two is company, four is a party, three is a crowd. One is a wanderer.

As he gets more drunk he remembers that morning's vow not to get drunk again tonight. Intoxication leads only into further reflection: "You're getting into one of those states that Marianne keeps telling you about, one of those states when people don't like to have you around." Finally he arrives at the center of the problem:

[1] Thurber, *The Middle-Aged Man on the Flying Trapeze* (New York, Harper and Row, 1935). Copr. © 1935 James Thurber; copr. © 1963 Helen W. Thurber and Rosemary Thurber Sauers.

Now look, the Mortons had said to him, if you and Marianne would only stop fighting and arguing and forever analyzing yourselves and forever analyzing everything, you'd be fine. You'd be fine if you got married and just shut up, just shut up and got married. That would be fine. Yes, sir, that would be fine. Everything would work out all right. You just shut up and get married, you just get married and shut up.

The repetitions in this monologue not only afford it dramatic intensity, but they also reflect his compulsive introspection. He cannot stop "analyzing everything", for, whatever discomfort the compulsion gives him, it nevertheless guards him from Kinstrey's fate. Even agonized awareness is preferable to the repression which leads to Kinstrey's destructive violence. Still, Kirk's situation is not enviable. Surrounded by people he knows, he cannot talk to any of them because he is so preoccupied with his loneliness, and none of them have anything to say to him which he can recognize as being relevant to his problems. Eventually, however, he must come to terms with himself, for, as things are, his difficulties can only increase.

The isolation of Jad Peters is far less self-conscious than Kirk's, but just as profound.[2] Jad, as a young man, had been prevented from boarding a certain ship by the last-minute arrival − so he said − of a telegram urging him home. The ship had gone down with all lives lost, and Jad was convinced that the intervention of God had spared him. From this point on, Jad began to see divine intervention in all aspects of his life; he "got so that he could figure out lucky escapes for himself in almost every disaster and calamity that happened in and around Sugar Grove". From each escape he preserved some souvenir which he kept on the coffee table at home. He became a sort of local character with his endlessly repeated stories.

I think Aunt Emma [Jad's wife] got so that she didn't hear Jad when he was talking, except on evenings when neighbors dropped in, and then she would have to take hold of the conversation and steer it away from any opening that might give Jad a chance to tell of some close escape he had had. But he always got his licks in. He would

[2] *The Middle-Aged Man on the Flying Trapeze*. Copr. © 1935 James Thurber; copr. © 1963 Helen W. Thurber and Rosemary Thurber Sauers.

bide his time, creaking back and forth in his chair, clicking his teeth, and not listening much to the talk about crops and begonias and the latest reports on the Spencer's feeble-minded child, and then, when there was a long pause, he would clear his throat and say that that reminded him of the time he had had a mind to go down to Pullen's lumber yard to fetch home a couple of two-by-fours to shore up the chicken house. Well, sir, he had pottered around the house a little while and was about to set out for Pullen's when something told him not to go a step. And it was that very day that a pile of lumber in the lumber yard let go and crushed Grant Pullen's leg so's it had to be amputated. Well sir, he would say – but Aunt Emma would cut in on him at this point. "Everybody's heard that old chestnut," she would say, with a forced little laugh, fanning herself in quick strokes with an old palm-leaf fan. Jad would go sullen and rock back and forth in his chair, clicking his teeth. He wouldn't get up when the guests rose to go – which they always did at this juncture. The memento of his close escape from the Pullen lumber-yard disaster was, of course, the chip of pine wood.

Aunt Emma is not the only member of the community who is contemptuous of Jad. The boys at Prentice's store, where Jad spends most of his time, amuse themselves at the old man's expense – even after his bizarre death (Jad had been struck by a huge rock which was hurled into town from the river where engineers were dynamiting; a moment before, he had turned around to say something to a friend):

I suppose old Jad hadn't been in his grave two days before the boys at Prentice's quit shaking their heads solemnly over the accident and began making funny remarks about it. Cal Gregg's was the funniest. "Well, sir," said Cal, "I don't suppose none of us will ever know what it was now, but somethin' must of told Jad to turn around."

Even worse than his friends' scorn is Aunt Emma's:

Aunt Emma had never liked [Jad] very much – she married him because he asked her to twice a week for seven years and because there had been nobody else she cared about; she stayed married to him on account of their children and because her people always stayed married.

And after Jad's death, Aunt Emma kept the rock that killed him on the coffee table with the rest of his souvenirs.

The isolation of the old man, as I have said, is as profound as

Kirk's. As Kirk is set off from his friends by his compulsive introspection, Jad is alienated by the force of imagination within him by which he makes these pathetic attempts to elevate himself in a community which despises him. In Ohio, at the turn of the century, imagination was tolerated only in women, who had nothing better to do with themselves; men were expected to be practical and to work hard. But Jad's story differs from Kirk's in an important respect. The reader is offered no relief from the latter's miseries; style and point of view combine to make "One is a Wanderer" one of Thurber's most effective despairing pieces. But "The Luck of Jad Peters" employs a narrator who mingles personal recollections of his aunt and uncle with reports from their neighbors he had known as a boy. Telling the story is an exercise in understanding for the narrator. He recalls,

When I was a little boy in the early nineteen-hundreds and was taken to Aunt Emma's house near Sugar Grove, Ohio, I used to wonder about [Jad's souvenirs].

After Jad's death, when Aunt Emma was asked about the rock on the table, she would say, " 'It's as much God's doing as that other cluttertrap.' " Aunt Emma's sister, "a very religious woman", would reply, " 'You can't taunt the Lord.' " This sister seems to represent one pole of the community's thought (the other is evident in the "boys" at Prentice's store):

I used to see [the sister] now and again at funerals, tall, gaunt, grim, but I never talked to her if I could help it. She liked funerals and she liked to look at corpses, and that made me afraid of her.

By the end the narrator understands the forces which made Jad's imagination manifest itself in eccentricity; at the end, the narrator comments ironically on the "funny remarks" made after Jad's death, and the irony implies rejection of this small-town world.

By contrast, the next two portraits to be examined, "Aunt Ida" and "Doc Marlowe", reveal imaginative individuals who avoided estrangement, and whose eccentricities were not damning. In "A Portrait of Aunt Ida", the narrator recalls a woman who dearly loved catastrophes, surgical operations, post-mortems, psychic foreshadowings, ghosts, and death.[3] Yet the amusement she takes in these preoccupations neither alarms nor offends people around her:

> She never saw in such things [as the *Titanic* disaster], as her older sisters, Emma and Clara did, the vengeance of a deity outraged by Man's lust for speed and gaiety; she looked for causes deep down in the dark heart of the corporate interests. You could never make her believe that the *Titanic* hit an iceberg ... the real cause she could not, or would not, make plain, but somewhere in its black core was a monstrous secret of treachery and corrupt goings-on – men were like that.

Eccentric as such illusions may be, they are not far enough from the unarticulated community stereotypes to alarm or offend the people around Aunt Ida. Nor is her identity so bound up in her fantasies (as Jad Peters' was) that she is incapable of relationships with real people. To the end of her ninety-one years she remained vital and a part of everything going on.

> Old Mrs. Kurtz, who is seventy-two, visited her on the last day, and when she left, Aunt Ida looked after her pityingly. "Poor Cora," she said, "she's failin', ain't she?"

It is, of course, partly because she is a woman that Aunt Ida's fantasies are tolerated. (In Thurber's world, women are instinctively attuned to society and to the universe.) Aunt Ida's imagination simply exaggerates things that most people believe to be basically true:

> Most of Aunt Ida's dreams foretold the fate of women, for what happened to women was of much greater importance to Aunt Ida than what happened to men. Men usually "brought things on themselves"; women, on the other hand, were usually victims of dark and devious goings-on of a more or less supernatural nature.

A man who would indulge his imagination, as Aunt Ida does, must either risk the alienation of Jad Peters or become a comedian; the second choice is explored by Doc Marlowe, who is surely one of Thurber's most engaging characters.

The narrator had been a boy when he first knew Doc, a Wild West medicine-show man.

[3] *The Middle-Aged Man on the Flying Trapeze.* Copr. © 1935 James Thurber; copr. © 1963 Helen W. Thurber and Rosemary Thurber Sauers.

He had been a lot of other things too: a circus man, the proprietor of a concession on Coney Island, a saloon-keeper. . . . When I first knew him, he represented the Wild West to me, and there was nobody I admired so much. . . . [He] wore scarred leather leggings, a bright-colored bead vest that he said he got from the Indians, and a ten-gallon hat with kitchen matches stuck in the band, all the way around. He was about six feet four inches tall, with big shoulders, and a long, drooping mustache. He let his hair grow long, like General Custer's. He had a wonderful collection of Indian relics and six shooters, and he used to tell me stories of his adventures in the Far West. . . . It wasn't until he died and his son came on from New Jersey for the funeral that I found out he had never been in the Far West in his life. He had been born in Brooklyn.[4]

As the portrait develops, the narrator recalls other disquieting things he discovered about his hero. Doc frequently played poker with his landlady and other boarders – and he always cheated. The narrator recalls his mixed anger and loyalty.

I knew I could never tell Mrs. Willoughby about how Doc had cheated her at seven-up. I liked her, but I liked him, too. Once he had given me a whole dollar to buy fireworks with on the Fourth of July.

On another occasion, Doc sold a dilapidated but "doctored" car to a family which had stayed with Mrs. Willoughby while stopping over in Columbus. The narrator is outraged at the deception and puzzled by Doc's amusement over the angry letter he gets from his victims.

As a boy, the narrator had been puzzled also about the medicine Doc sold. The ingredients were well-known, standard and expensive, and Doc sold his "ointment" for little more than it cost him. At various times he "treated" people for nothing and sometimes cured them. As a man, the narrator has come to realize that Doc sold, not liniment, but confidence; thus he was able to remain a part of a community which valued a "faith-healer" as highly as a physician. But more important, the narrator, in maturity, sees that Doc's confidence games provided exercise for a vigorous imagination and amusement for a life

---

[4] *Let Your Mind Alone!* (New York, Harper and Row, 1937). Copr. © 1937 James Thurber; copr. © 1965 Helen W. Thurber and Rosemary Thurber Sauers.

which would otherwise have been intolerably tedious. As he was dying, Doc gave the narrator a two-headed quarter:

"Never let the other fella call the turn, Jimmy, my boy," said Doc, with a shadow of his old twinkle and the echo of his old chuckle. I still have the two-headed quarter. For a long time I didn't like to think about it, or about Doc Marlowe, but I do now.

The theme of the story is similar to Sherwood Anderson's "I Want to Know Why", but where that story ends on a note of disillusionment, Thurber's goes beyond to the successful reconciliation of past and present. Doc is no longer a hero, but instead is something far more real – that is, he is a man. The boy's disillusionment has been transformed into understanding and acceptance of both Doc and his world. When the narrator tells at the end that now he likes to think about Doc and the trick coin, we see that he "knows why".

As Doc Marlowe was a kind of comedian, so Thurber himself becomes in the stories of his family which compose *My Life and Hard Times*.[5] We are never quite allowed to forget that Thurber's hilarious family derived from the same culture which produced such an alien as Jad Peters. But where Jad's imagination contributed to his isolation, the characters in *My Life* are bound together in a comic world in which no one is normal, but where everyone is having a good time, and seems deeply involved with other people. At least one critic has called Thurber's family a "collection of psychotics", and certainly there is an element of madness.[6] However, the generalization does not very accurately define Thurber's characters, for it applies equally well to the citizens of Winesburg, Ohio. Anderson demonstrated that the subconscious operates toward the disintegration of personality in a repressive community. Thurber's characters, as self-conscious clowns, sometimes avert madness and find integrity in humor.

An incident in "The Car We Had to Push" affords a capsule

[5] *My Life and Hard Times* (New York, Harper and Row, 1933). Copr. © 1933, 1961 James Thurber.
[6] Norris Yates, *The American Humorist* (Ames, Iowa, Iowa State University Press, 1964), p. 275.

glimpse of the world of *My Life*. The narrator tells us that, like his father, he was ignorant and suspicious of early automobiles. The car of the title is an old Reo which could no longer be started by the crank. "My father used to get sick at his stomach pushing the car, and very often was unable to go to work." The only car that interests the narrator belonged to the Get-Ready Man, "a lank unkempt elderly gentleman with wild eyes and a deep voice who used to go about shouting at people through a megaphone to prepare for the end of the world. 'GET READY! GET READ-Y' he would bellow." The narrator remembers the time the Get-Ready Man participated in a performance of *King Lear* – from the balcony.

Neither father nor I, who were there, ever completely got over the scene, which went something like this:

EDGAR:	Tom's a-cold. – o, do de, do de, do de! – Bless thee from whirlwinds, star-blasting, and taking . . . the foul fiend vexes! *(Thunder off.*
LEAR:	What! Have his daughters brought him to this pass? –
GET-READY MAN:	Get Ready! Get Ready!
EDGAR:	Pillicock sat on Pillicock-hill – Halloo, Halloo, loo, loo! *(Lightning flashes.*
GET-READY MAN:	The Worllld is com-ing to an end!
FOOL:	This cold night will turn us all to fools and madmen!

Thurber's Columbus is nearly a mirror image of Lear's England. Father is certainly the sanest member of the family, but he is, as we shall see, estranged from and victimized by, his sons and wife, in a home where madness is normal. The Fool's comment seems to be the aspect of the scene which the narrator never "completely got over". In a world where imagination threatens insanity, and where sanity leads to sickness and alienation, some-how a balance must be struck. As the Fool has the most com-prehensive overview in *Lear,* so the narrator of *My Life* learns to become a clown, that he not fall in looking at his world.

What Father never "completely got over" was the more ob-vious threat of madness intruding upon the sane and dignified world in which people go to the theater to see Shakespeare performed. Thurber's version of *Lear* is probably not superior to Shakespeare's, but it is certainly funnier. The humor, though, is undoubtedly lost on Father, just as the humor of various practical jokes his sons play is not appreciated. There was, for example, the "little scheme of Roy's to frighten father, who had always thought the car might explode". The youngest son had suspended a huge collection of kitchen utensils underneath the car, and when they were driving about, he released them onto the street with a "lingering, clamant crash".

"Stop the *car*!" shouted father. "I can't," Roy said. "The engine fell out." "God Almighty!" said father, who knew what that meant, or knew what it sounded as if it might mean.

The incident ends – "unhappily", the narrator says – when they have to drive back to pick up the pieces; even Father can tell the difference between an automobile engine and an egg-beater.

In another story, "More Alarms at Night", both Roy and the narrator besiege Father. Roy, who has been sick in bed, pretends one night to have been overcome by delirium.

He got out of bed and, going to my father's room, shook him and said, "Buck, your time has come!" My father's name was not Buck but Charles, nor had he ever been called Buck. He was a tall, mildly nervous, peaceable gentleman, given to quiet pleasures, and eager that everything should run smoothly. "Hmm?" he said, with drowsy bewilderment. "Get up, Buck," said my brother, coldly, but with a certain gleam in his eyes. My father leaped out of bed, on the side away from his son, rushed from the room, locked the door behind him, and shouted us all up.

Mother accuses Father of having had a bad dream and when they go back to look at Roy, the boy seems fast asleep in his own bed. Only Father and Roy know what really happened, and Father is scolded:

My mother declared that it was "a sin and a shame" for a grown man to wake up a sick boy simply because he (the grown man: father) had got on his back and had a bad dream.

A few months later the narrator has insomnia one night and cannot remember the name of a certain town in New Jersey

(Perth Amboy). He begins to fear he is losing his mind, so plagued is he with irrelevant associations, and suddenly determines that he must talk to someone else and find the elusive name. He awakens his father: " 'Listen,' I said. "Name some towns in New Jersey quick!' " Father can only assume that another son has gone suddenly crazy; he leaps from his bed and runs for the door, shouting to arouse the others. The narrator grapples with his father and together they shout. When Mother comes, she is fully equal to the situation:

"*Now* what?" demanded my mother, grimly, pulling us apart. She was capable, fortunately, of handling any two of us and she never in her life was alarmed by the words or actions of any of us.

This time both victim and assailant are scolded and sent back to bed.

Father's inability to deal with the circumstances of his home are neatly illustrated in the scene which ends "The Car We Had to Push". The car had been parked too near the trolley tracks one night and had been demolished. The ensuing commotion upest Grandfather who was, at the time, refighting the Civil War. Grandfather assumes that the fuss about the car refers to the death of some person, and eventually he decides that it must be about his brother Zenas, who, long ago, "caught the same disease that was killing the chestnut trees in those years and passed away". The old man becomes extremely difficult: "He would go into towering rages in which he threatened to call the Board of Health unless the funeral were held at once." Father persuades a friend to dress in the style of the 1860s and pretend to be Zenas, but the scheme works no better than any other of Father's.

The newcomer held out both his hands. "Clem!" he cried to grandfather. Grandfather turned slowly, looked at the intruder, and snorted. "Who air *you*?" he demanded in his deep, resonant voice. "I'm Zenas!" cried Martin. "Your brother Zenas, fit as a fiddle and sound as a dollar!" "Zenas, my foot!" said grandfather. "Zenas died of the chestnut blight in '66!"

Grandfather is the most unpredictable factor in Thurber's early world (just as Father is its most sane and reliable citizen), and the old man's greatest moment comes in "The Night the Ghost Got In". The narrator has just got out of the bathtub when he hears footsteps downstairs. He goes to the stairway and peers down but sees nothing; his older brother, Herman, joins him and together they hear the steps start up the stairs, but still see nothing. At this point they slam the door and this arouses Mother, who assumes that the commotion was caused by burglars. The police are called and after they break down the front door, search through the house. Of course they find nothing, but while talking to the family on the second floor, they hear the creaking of Grandfather's bed in the attic.

Five or six cops sprang for the attic door before I could intervene or explain. I realized that it would be bad if they burst in on grandfather unannounced, or even announced. He was going through a phase in which he believed that General Meade's men, under steady hammering by Stonewall Jackson, were beginning to retreat and even desert.

No five or six cops are a match for the old man

"Back, ye cowardly dogs!" roared grandfather. "Back 't the lines, ye goddam lily-livered cattle!" With that he fetched the officer who found the zither a flat-handed smack alongside his head that sent him sprawling. The others beat a retreat, but not fast enough; grandfather grabbed Zither's gun from its holster and let fly. The report seemed to crack the rafters; smoke filled the attic. A cop cursed and shot his hand to his shoulder. Somehow, we all finally got downstairs again and locked the door against the old gentleman.

The cops leave reluctantly, after the narrator has promised to return the gun next day, aware that "the night had been distinctly a defeat for them". Grandfather has the last word next morning:

Over his third cup of coffee, he glared at Herman and me. "What was the idee of all them cops tarryhootin' round the house last night?" he demanded. He had us there.

At the outbreak of World War I, Grandfather, with visions of leading a division into Germany, tries to enlist. "He applied several times and each time he took off his coat and threatened to whip the men who said he was too old." At this point, the old man begins to talk of "going over to Lancaster, his old home town, and putting his problem to 'Cump' – that is, General William Tecumseh Sherman, also an old Lancaster boy". In this, as in his shooting of the policeman, Grandfather's madness goes over the border into a country which the narrator does not wish to visit. Like the Get-Ready Man, Grandfather asserts his integrity in his battle against the rest of the world, but at the price of only occasionally perceiving reality. Both old men have constructed worlds of their own, and these worlds, as we have seen in "The Whip-poor-will", "The Secret Life of Walter Mitty", and "One is a Wanderer", afford no very great security to a "modern" man – which the narrator is to become.

Grandfather, however, is not the only lunatic in the family; nearly all the women we see suffer delusions. In "The Night the Bed Fell", we are told of Aunt Sarah Shoaf –

... who never went to bed at night without the fear that a burglar was going to get in and blow chloroform under her door through a tube. To avert this calamity – for she was in greater dread of anesthetics than of losing her household goods – she always piled her money, silverware and other valuables in a neat stack just outside her bedroom, with a note reading: "This is all I have. Please take it and do not use your chloroform, as this is all I have."

Aunt Gracie Shoaf, however, meets her burglar problem "with more fortitude". She would pile all the household's shoes by the bedroom door and when she heard the burglars – every night – she would throw shoes down the hallway at them. "Some nights she threw them all, some nights only a couple of pair." And in "The Night the Ghost Got In", Mother also threw a shoe from her bedroom window through the neighbor's window in order to have them call the police (since the Thurbers' telephone is downstairs with the "burglars").

After [the neighbors] had disappeared from the window, mother suddenly made as if to throw another shoe, not because there was further need of it, but, as she later explained, because the thrill of heaving a shoe through a window glass had enormously taken her fancy. I prevented her.

In "The Car We Had to Push" we learn of some of Mother's delusions regarding mechanical things.

[She] thought – or, rather, knew – that it was dangerous to drive an automobile without gasoline: it fried the valves or something. "Now don't you dare drive all over town without gasoline!" she would say to us when we started off.

She also dreaded the Victrola which "might blow up".

It alarmed her, rather than reassured her, to explain that the phonograph was run neither by gasoline nor by electricity.

During storms she would take the telephone receiver off the hook and let it hang. *Her* mother "lived the latter years of her life in the horrible suspicion that electricity was dripping invisibly all over the house".

It leaked, she contended, out of empty sockets if the wall switch had been left on. She would go around screwing in bulbs, and if they lighted up she would hastily and fearfully turn off the wall switch and go back to her *Pearson's* or *Everybody's*, happy in the satisfaction that she had stopped not only a costly but a dangerous leakage.

The narrator, as I have said, is forced to adopt values which lie somewhere between the sanity and dignity of his father, the lunacy of his grandfather, and the delusions of his mother. He is endowed with the kind of imagination which precludes becoming a "peaceable gentleman, given to quiet pleasures, and eager that everything should run smoothly" – as he has described his father. But instead of sharing the delusions of his mother, regarding mechanical things, he makes them the source of comedy. In describing the death of the old Reo, he reveals the kind of imaginative control he exercises over his world:

The first streetcar that came along couldn't get by. It picked up the tired old automobile as a terrier might seize a rabbit and drubbed it unmercifully, losing its hold now and then but catching a new grip a second later. Tires booped and whooshed, the fenders queeled and graked, the steering-wheel rose up like a spectre and disappeared in the direction of Franklin Avenue with a melancholy whistling sound, bolts and gadgets flew like sparks from a Catherine wheel.

But not only is the author of *My Life and Hard Times* a comedian, the involved narrator also takes that role. As the policemen who investigated the ghost-burglar are about to leave, a reporter, who had accompanied them, questions the narrator (who is dressed no longer in his bath towel, but in "one of mother's blouses, not being able to find anything else".

The reporter looked at me with mingled suspicion and interest. "Just what the hell is the real lowdown here, Bud?" he asked. I decided to be frank with him. "We had ghosts," I said. He gazed at me a long time as if I were a slot machine into which he had, without results, dropped a nickel. Then he walked away.

By the time the narrator enters the university, he has learned enough to deal with both madness and uncoping sanity. In "University Days" his inability to see plant-cells through a microscope enrages his botany professor. The narrator tries his best, but only once does he find anything but a "nebulous milky substance – a phenomenon of mal-adjustment". "That time I saw, to my pleasure and amazement, a variegated constellation of flecks, specks, and dots."

"You didn't, you didn't, you *did*n't!" [the professor] screamed, losing control of his temper instantly, and he bent over and squinted into the microscope. His head snapped up. "That's your eye!" he shouted. "You've fixed the lens so that it reflects! You've drawn your eye!"

The professor's career seems to depend on Thurber's seeing the cells:

"As God is my witness, I'll arrange this glass so that you see cells through it or I'll give up teaching. In twenty-two years of botany, I – " . . . he genuinely wished to hold onto his temper; his scenes with me had taken a great deal out of him.

There is no capacity in the man simply to recognize that someone might not be able to adjust a microscope. For his part, though, the narrator seems to regard the beauty of his own eye as of equal importance to the beauty of plant cells. An education about one's self seems more important to the narrator than an education which looks only toward the outside world, and the value of such an education is revealed in this very incident: flunking botany is not so serious a blow to him as to his professor.

Again, in "Draft Board Nights", the narrator is equal to the harrassment of bureaucratic inefficiency. The first time he is called up for examination, he is told that his vision is too poor for him to serve. Almost every week, until the armistice, he receives a letter ordering him to report for his physical – and each time he is exempted.

The ninth or tenth time I was called, I happened to pick up one of several stethoscopes that were lying on a table and suddenly, instead of finding myself in the line of draft men, I found myself in the line of examiners. "Hello, doctor," said one of them, nodding. "Hello," I said.... I was assigned, or rather drifted, to the chest-and-lung section, where I began to examine every other man, thus cutting old Dr. Ridgeway's work in two. "I'm glad to have you here, doctor," he said.

For the next four months he "served" with the draft board as an examiner, but for his last few trips, he again became a draft prospect, having grown tired of the other.

The control exercised by the narrator of *My Life and Hard Times* over his world is a fair indication of the value of his education in preparing him for modern life. In the Preface, Thurber apologetically compares his own lack of achievement to Cellini's dictum that an autobiographer "should have accomplished something of excellence". Writers of short, humorous pieces, however, "sit on the edge of the chair of literature. In the house of life they have the feeling that they have never taken off their overcoat."

... they stick to short accounts of their misadventures because they never get so deep into them but that they feel they can get out.... To call such persons "humorists," a loose-fitting and ugly word, is to miss the nature of their dilemma and the dilemma of their nature. The little wheels of their invention are set in motion by the hands of melancholy.

He remembers what Ford Madox Ford called "the sole reason for writing one's memoirs: namely to paint a picture of one's time".

Your short piece writer's time is not Walter Lippmann's time, or Stuart Chase's time, or Professor Einstein's time. It is his own personal time, circumscribed by the short boundaries of his pain and his embarrassment, in which what happens to his digestion, the rear axle of his car, and the confused flow of his relationships with six or eight persons and two or three buildings is of greater importance than what goes on in the nation or in the universe.

But no apology is needed. If Thurber has failed to discover the large principles and systems by which contemporary problems can be solved, he has, instead, discovered that life's generalities are somehow of less value than its particulars. It is only when principles of virtue and honor are discarded that Doc Marlowe can be admired and loved, instead of worshipped. Father in his dignity has never learned that the importance he attaches to dignity causes him to become ill when the car will not start, and prevents him from coping with the goings-on of his household. The comedian learns early, as Thurber has said elsewhere, that human dignity is "not only silly but a little sad".[7] Lacking humor, the plight of modern man is Kirk's; but the comedian is more capable than Kirk of dealing with things as they are, less driven to wander the streets, to wander in his own mind. Where Kirk is too much in the middle of things to see well, the comedian can at once stand in the middle – in his bath towel – and above – supervising.

---

[7]   Quoted in Max Eastman, *Enjoyment of Laughter* (New York, Simon and Schuster, 1936), p. 343.

V

FABLE AND FAIRY TALE

The artist's compulsion to transform imaginatively his experience
before giving it artistic form often drives Thurber beyond the
representational, and into the land of romance visited previously
by Hawthorne and Melville and by Lewis Carroll. Here, fiction
is represented by its most basic and unpretentious form, the
simple fable. But the artist's fable is both more realistic and more
fantastic than the folk fable. In Thurber's fables, the relationships
between the conscious and unconscious, the real and the imaginary, are more subtle and complex, less precisely defined, than
in his representational fiction. These stories are apt to end in
confusion rather than clarity, yet the confusion reflects what has
been in the character's or persona's experience; paradoxically,
such confusion leaves the reader with a more integrated and a
clearer sense of that experience.

Fantasy is of course a major part of Thurber's representational
work, as every reader of "The Secret Life of Walter Mitty" recalls. But the fantastic, which is so important a part of his fables,
differs from that in his "naturalistic" stories in at least two important respects. First, in the representational work, the reader
is rarely in doubt about what is imaginary and what is actual;
Mitty's dreams are readily distinguishable from the real world he
inhabits. In the fables, however, there is a continuously shifting
relationship between the real and fantastic; things are seldom
what they seem. Second, dreams mark the limits of awareness
and of imagination for realistic characters; but in the fable,
fantasy allows the artist to achieve what has been called "super-
realism" – the fantastic exaggeration and distortion of appearance

as a means of representing both the matter and essence of reality.[1]
It is this which enables the artist to control his world, to become
the single artificer of the world he sings. To this end, style becomes an extremely important element in the making of comedy.

The fables we shall consider here can be divided into three
rough categories. The first group includes the very short items in
Fables for Our Time and *Further Fables for Our Time.* In the
second group are pieces which begin as if they were indeed
representational stories, but in which strange and wondrous
things happen – pieces such as "Mr. Preble Gets Rid of His
Wife", "A Box to Hide In", and "Back to the Grades".[2] The third
category – and perhaps the most interesting – is Thurber's fairy
tales: *Many Moons, The Great Quillow, The White Deer, The
13 Clocks,* and *The Wonderful O.* Of these latter, the first three
will be examined in some detail.

In his "Parable in Pictures", *The Last Flower* (1939), Thurber
so closely combines pathos and farce that one doesn't know, at
the end, whether to laugh or cry. The concrete details of the
prose fables are here provided in the drawing – though fully to
describe these would take more space than can be allowed.
Created just as World War II was breaking out in Europe, the
series of drawings begins with the collapse of civilization following World War XII. Cities, forests, gardens and works of art
have been dessicated; malevolent-looking birds hang in the air
over tilting church steeples, broken statuary, shattered trees, and
the desolate, naked people. The few survivors are dying out and
the race would have become extinct except that a young girl
happened upon the last flower left in the world. She tried to tell
the others about it, but no one cared; finally a young man went
with her and together they nurtured it. Before long there were

---

[1]   The term seems to have been coined by Herbert Read: see "Surrealism
and the Romantic Principle", in the specially revised version which appears in M. Schorer, J. Miles, and G. McKenzie, eds., *Criticism* (New York,
1958), p. 95.
[2]   These stories are collected in *The Middle-Aged Man on the Flying
Trapeze* (New York, Harper and Row, 1935). Copr. © 1935 James
Thurber; copr. © 1963 Helen W. Thurber and Rosemary Thurber Sauers.

many flowers and then the young man and woman discovered each other and "love was reborn into the world". Soon the man put one stone on top of another, and then civilization was re-established; but along with the tailors and cobblers, painters and poets, came soldiers and then liberators who, "under the guidance of God, set fire to the discontent" which accompanied the re-development of culture and society. Presently there was another war, and "This time the destruction was so complete that nothing at all was left in the world except one man and one woman and one flower."

It seems almost less horrible to know that one will die, than to know that life may go on – and on, and on. In this fable, Thurber's despair at the failure of civilization is stripped to its barest possible form – a fact echoed by the naked figures in the drawings. Yet it is a "parable" and this itself suggests a glimmer of hope that perhaps, somehow, the next civilization may learn from the errors of the present one. Thurber's dedication of the book to his daughter is integral: "In the wistful hope that her world will be better than mine." The fable, the parable, always seek to teach; the very form implies a concern with the future, and thus, hope, however faint. The drawings too, in contrast with the grimness of the text, force us to feel, by their caricature and exaggeration, not only folly but humor as well. Here, as in the other fables, humor affords at least slight protection against our consciousness of the Awful.

Perhaps the most familiar of Thurber's prose fables is "The Unicorn in the Garden". When the husband sees a unicorn quietly cropping roses in the garden, he goes upstairs to tell his wife; she reacts like any Thurber woman: " 'The unicorn is a mythical beast.' " The wife declares that she will have her husband put into a "booby-hatch" – a word he dislikes – and when he goes back to the garden, she calls a psychiatrist and the police. But when they come, she is the one they carry off, for as the husband tells them, " 'The unicorn is a mythical beast.' " In this, as in many of his fables, Thurber achieves much of his comedy by playing with the very conventions by which a fable can exist. The reader willingly suspends disbelief long enough to agree at the beginning that this husband might very well have seen a unicorn in his garden. But immediately we are thrown back into the world in which unicorns do not exist, and at the end we are not certain whether the husband actually saw one, whether it was a delusive symbol for whatever imaginative things give him a "high heart", or whether he simply invented the tale to annoy his wife. Yet we are not allowed simply to ignore these problems as irrelevant to the fable, and here lies the principal difference between Thurber's fables and Aesop's: where the latter illustrates simplified concepts with his beast stories, Thurber reverses the process, using the fable as a means of demonstrating complexity.

The conjunction of the real and the imaginary lends to "The Unicorn in the Garden" a dream-like quality that lifts it above either naturalism or fable. But it is difficult to regard so brief a piece as a work of art: art seems to require a fuller development. It is in the longer stories which seem both representational and fabulous that Thurber is able to create a truly super-realistic art; such pieces combine disciplined development with imaginative freedom. "A Box to Hide In", for example, begins in the manner of any number of "realistic" tales:

I waited till the large woman with the awful hat took up her sack of groceries and went out, peering at the tomatoes and lettuce on her way. The clerk asked me what mine was.

"Have you got a box," I asked, "a large box? I want a box to hide in."

Until the last sentence, we have no clue that there is to be anything out of the ordinary here. But at this point, the narrative seems to enter another realm, where, within the mind, things are said that are not said: what Thurber man would add such an explanation to a grocery clerk? The performance is repeated when a clerk in another store asks, " 'Whatta you mean you want to hide in this box?' "

"It's a form of escape," I told him, "hiding in a box. It circumscribes your worries and the range of your anguish. You don't see people, either."

The clerk is immediately concerned with practical problems:

"How in the hell do you eat when you're in this box?"... I said I had never been in a box and didn't know, but that would take care of itself....

It was the same everyplace. I gave up when it got dark and the groceries closed, and hid in my room again. I turned out the light and lay on the bed. You feel better when it gets dark. I could have hid in a closet. Nobody pays any attention to a big box lying on the floor. You could stay in it for days and nobody'd think to look in it, not even the cleaning-woman.

From the notion that eating "would take care of itself", and from the very nature of the box, we can surmise that the narrator, like Macduff, had been "ripp'd untimely" from his mother, and would return to a place where his security is not threatened by the "real" world.

When the cleaning-woman comes next morning the narrator asks her if she knows of a box big enough to hide in.

She looked at me with big, dim eyes. There's something wrong with her glands. She's awful but she has a big heart, which makes it worse. She's unbearable, her husband is sick, and her children are sick and she is sick too. I got to thinking how pleasant it would be if I were in a box now, and didn't have to see her.

The fantasy begins to assume concrete form:

I wondered if you have a desire to bark or laugh when someone who doesn't know walks by the box you are in. Maybe she would have a spell with her heart, if I did that, and would die right there. The officers and the elevatorman and Mrs. Gramadge would find us.

When the narrator's fantasy ends, "It was hard to realize that she wasn't dead." Still the cleaning-woman looks at him dully. The narrator resigns himself to reality.

I haven't found one yet, but I still have this overpowering urge to hide in a box. Maybe it will go away, maybe I'll be all right. Maybe it will get worse. It's hard to say.

The "awfulness" of the cleaning-woman and the practicality of the grocery clerk are apparently aspects of the world which threaten the narrator; both his conversations with the clerks and the fantasy of "murdering" the cleaning-woman reveal the anger which makes the narrator want to hide. Yet at the end we are not certain whether the questions were ever asked, whether or not they too might have been fantasies.

"Mr. Preble Gets Rid of His Wife" begins, as do all these stories, in a quite ordinary way.

Mr. Preble was a plump middle-aged lawyer in Scarsdale. He used to kid with his stenographer about running away with him. "Let's run away together," he would say, during a pause in dictation. "All righty," she would say.

One rainy Monday afternoon, Mr. Preble was more serious about it than usual. . . .

"My wife would be glad to get rid of me," he said.

"Would she give you a divorce?" asked the stenographer.

"I don't suppose so," he said. The stenographer laughed.

"You'd have to get rid of your wife," she said.

After dinner that night he tries to persuade his wife to go down into the cellar and she refuses. They bicker, in the manner of Thurber couples:

"Gee whiz!" said Mr. Preble, kicking at the edge of the rug. "Other people's wives go down in the cellar. Why is it you never want to do anything? I come home worn out from the office and you won't even go down in the cellar with me. God knows it isn't very far – it isn't as if I was asking you to go to the movies or some place."

"I don't want to *go!*" shouted Mrs. Preble. Mr. Preble sat down on the edge of a davenport.

In the "Gee whiz" and the kicking at the rug, Mr. Preble seems like a small boy asking a favor of mother. Mrs. Preble continues to refuse until her husband finally tells her that he really wants to run off with his stenographer. He does not tell his wife that he wants to kill her, but she replies,

"I knew all along you wanted to get me down there and bury me."

"You can say that now – after I told you," said Mr. Preble. "But it would never have occurred to you if I hadn't."

"You didn't tell me; I got it out of you," said Mrs. Preble. "Anyway, I'm always two steps ahead of what you're thinking."

The mother-child relationship is heightened here; it is mother who always knows what one is thinking about. She chides his inability to carry out his plan and assumes that his stenographer had put him up to it. Furthermore, if he did bury her, he would undoubtedly "blab it to the whole world. . . . Why don't you go to bed? You're just getting yourself all worked up over nothing."

Finally Mrs. Preble agrees to go down to the cellar, just to "have a little peace". The cellar is cold and she complains, "Any other husband would have buried his wife in the summer." When he is about to hit her with a shovel, she nags, "Do you want to leave a great big clue right here in the middle of everything where the first detective that comes snooping around will find it? Go out in the street and find some piece of iron or something." He is sure he won't be able to find anything, but she replies,

"If you look in the right place you'll find it," said Mrs. Preble. "And don't be gone long. Don't you dare stop in the cigar store. I'm not going to stand down here in this cold cellar all night and freeze."

"All right," said Mr. Preble. "I'll hurry."

"And shut that *door* behind you!" she screamed after him. "Where were you born – in a barn?"

Thus the story ends. There is no clue anyplace that the conversation and events described are not actual, yet the story makes sense only if we regard everything following the dialogue with the stenographer as fantasy. Mr. Preble is caught between his emotional dependence on his wife, and his sense that he really should be free of her. Regarded this way, the story reflects both previous experience with his wife, and also his need for her nagging presence. Like so many Thurber husbands, he is incapable of dealing with her and incapable of doing without her; the confusion in his mind is reflected in the story's refusal to be either naturalistic or fanciful.

Perhaps the most complex of these super-realistic stories – next to the fairy tales which will be discussed later – is "Back to the Grades". This piece begins as a spoof on famous executives who boast of having started their careers "shoveling in the boiler room". The narrator recalls that at "thirty-four going on thirty-five" he returned to grammar school.

One evening after we had returned from a contract-bridge game, my wife said to me, earnestly: "You ought to go back to the fifth grade." I suggested just as earnestly that she, too, should start over again, beginning with the first grade (she is younger than I am), but we finally compromised on my going back to the fifth grade.

He goes to live with his parents when he returns to grammar school and the old relationships are re-established.

The first morning of school, I couldn't find my hat. "If you'd hang up your hat, you'd know where it was," my mother said. "Let him find it himself; don't you hunt for it," said my father. I finally found it in the dog house with my baseball glove.

In school he has the same teacher he had had twenty-five years before, and she punishes him for being late to class ("I was used to staying up until one and two o'clock in the morning. I never go to sleep at ten").

I was so bad at problems that I had to stay after class and clean the blackboard-erasers. It was fun leaning out the window and slapping them against the wall of the building; the chalk spurted like smoke from a gun and got into your nose, and the erasers left little white rectangles on the bricks. Afterwards I drew a picture of Miss Malloy on the blackboard and went home.

He brings some applejack to Miss Malloy, who stays after school to help him with his "problems", but she gets soused and he decides to have his father help him; this is too much for Father:

"I don't propose to go through the fifth grade again at my age!" said Father, vehemently. Grandfather was furious. "You git your chores done and hike on to school or I'll whup your hide off!" he shouted at Father. We had to change the subject.

Father prevails and the narrator has to drop out. Or, rather, he is kicked out for pulling the hair of the little girl who sits in front of him.

Miss Malloy came down the aisle and hit me across the hand with a ruler. I took the ruler away from her, sat on top of my desk, turned her over my knee, and spanked her.

The tale concludes:

My analyst (who is losing ground steadily) told me later that it was a happy thing that I had been able to go back to school and spank my teacher. He said that noticeably good results would begin to show up in my life. They haven't, though.

Even the ending, which suggests that the whole matter was a dream, doesn't really clarify the relationship between fantasy and reality in the story. We can be no more certain that spanking the teacher was imaginary, than that there really is an analyst. What we can recognize, however, is that there is an attempt in this story to reconcile the narrator's past failure with present reality; but the latter includes not only personal shortcomings but also a world for which his education did not prepare him. Had he learned, as a child, "sentence-parsing, fractions, decimals, long division", he might not feel unable to understand "taxation, gas-meter readings, endowment or straight-pay insurance", and so forth.

Nor could I get much meaning out of the books and articles which were being written all the time on economics and politics. Long stretches of Walter Lippmann meant nothing to me.

The "present" of the story is 1929-1930 – the first years of the depression, and nothing in the fifth grade or any other grade could have adapted anyone for the world war, the economic disaster, or the preparation in Europe for another war. In such a world it seems as irrelevant to revisit the past and establish mature relationship with persons formerly in authority, as it does to start all over with fractions. And yet, it is all an individual can do.

In "Back to the Grades", as in the two stories previously discussed, the juxtaposition of the real and the imaginary renders the theme more completely than would be possible in a more naturalistic story; consider these two views of the teacher:

"Don't cramp your fingers; get a free and easy wrist motion," Miss Malloy said. "Aw," I said, and grinned. She told me to wipe the smile off my face. I wouldn't, and she made me learn "To a Waterfowl" by heart.

A paragraph later the narrator is staying after school again.

"I'll ask my father to help me with the problems," I said one after-noon, when, at the end of an hour, I hadn't gotten anywhere and neither had Miss Malloy – except with the applejack. Miss Malloy didn't say anything. She looked at me. "Fines' fatha ev' had," she said. "Fines' probblums ev' solve, too." She began to cry and I went home.

It is this kind of juxtaposition that enables Thurber to transform the simple fairy tale into literary statement which is almost without precedent in the genre. In these we will see that most of the devices already discussed in connection with the brief fables are employed. However, further comment concerning the function of puns and alliteration in Thurber's comic style is called for at this point. Thurber has been attacked at least once for the "trivia" which seems to dominate much of his work – the word is used to describe the "word-game" pieces. But Thurber asks, "Which is trivia – the diamond or the elephant?" [3] And in "The Tyranny of Trivia" he argues that preoccupation with minutiae can be a means of living with the Awful without losing awareness of the details of existence, hence reality. That is, the words seem to lose much of their symbolic quality and are transformed by the imagination into real things:

> Most of the characters in B . . . murder sleep: the bugler, braggart, blowhard, blatherskite, barber, blower, barker, booster, bouncer, bruiser, and so on. But their broken-bottle barroom brawling, bombast, bluster, and blockbusting bombardment of Babel and Bedlam die down when you come upon the subdued figures of the only truly quiet characters in the second letter of the alphabet – the butler, the bridegroom and the burglar. The first night I came upon them, whispering and tiptoeing in the corridors of B, I fell asleep almost instantly.[4]

The humor in these catalogues can become tiresome, especially when they go on for many, many pages, but their importance, as a clue to the kind and quality of Thurber's imagination, cannot be exaggerated.

Perhaps this can be seen more clearly in connection with a series of drawings he once did, *A New Natural History*.[5] Here,

---

[3] The attack is made by Otto Friedrich in the 1955 issue of *Discovery*, which I have not been able to obtain; Thurber alludes to at in the beginning of "The Tyranny of Trivia", in *Lanterns and Lances* (New York, 1961), p. 75. The reply quoted in my text is made to the *Paris Review* interviewers.

[4] "The Tyranny of Trivia"; see note 3 above.

[5] *The Beast in Me and Other Animals* (New York, Harcourt, Brace and World, 1948), p. 151. Copr. © 1948 James Thurber.

words become the flora and fauna of a wilderness penetrated by one explorer only. There is the trochee – a cat-like beast, whose body slopes abruptly upwards from very short hind legs to long forelegs – facing a Spondee – a straight-backed cat, otherwise similar to the Trochee. There is the White-faced Rage (a dog-headed rodent with a black body) and the Blind Rage (eyeless). And there is the Lapidary in a clump of Merry-Go-Round – a beast with a camel's head on a long neck attached to a very small horse's body, standing in a clump of small round flowers. The Goad, the Apothecary, the Great Gatsby (a butterfly), the Scout-master, the Barred Barrister – there seems no end to Thurber's inventiveness, nor to his compulsion to render the transformations of experience. It is a usual thing in fables to attribute human characteristics to animals; Thurber seems nearly to reverse this, to transform the symbols of human communication into animals.

As I have suggested above, Thurber finds an adequate frame-work for these verbal pyrotechnics in his fairy tales. These tales, as Edmund Wilson has said, mark Thurber's "rapid elimination of the last vestiges of the conventional humorist and his emer-gence as a comic artist of the top layer of our contemporary writing".[6] The first of these, *Many Moons*,[7] is perhaps most nearly a conventional fairy tale, but even here the elements which lift the later tales above the normal standards for such things are present. It begins, "Once upon a time, in a kingdom by the sea", and tells the story of a little Princess, Lenore, who was sick in bed. The King promises her anything she wants, and she replies, "I want the moon. If I can have the moon I will be well again." But neither the Lord High Chamberlain, the Royal Wizard, nor the Royal Mathematician can get the moon for her; each of them tells the King the moon is a different distance from earth, a different size, and of a different composition – though in all cases, it is unobtainable. The Court Jester tells the King, "They are all wise men ... and so they must all be right." But

6   "Books", *The New Yorker*, 21 (October 27, 1945), p. 86.
7   Thurber, *Many Moons* (New York, Harcourt, Brace and World, 1943). Copr. © 1943 James Thurber.

at this point, the reader's acceptance of magic, his willing suspension, is turned upon him to comic effect; the Jester continues,

"If they are all right, then the moon must be just as large and as far
away as each person thinks it is. The thing to do is find out how
big Princess Lenore thinks it is, and how far away."

The moon, according to Lenore, is "just a little smaller than my
thumbnail . . . for when I hold my thumbnail up at the moon, it
just covers it." Also it is "not as high as the big tree outside my
window", and it is made of gold. It is an easy matter for the
Jester to have the Royal Goldsmith make a moon for Lenore,
and immediately she gets well. But a new problem arises, for
what will happen when Lenore sees the moon rise over her tree
again that night? None of the royal wisemen can give the king a
solution, but when the moon does rise, the Jester goes to the
Princess and asks her how it can be that there are two moons:

"That's easy, silly," she said. "When I lose a tooth, a new one grows
in its place, doesn't it?"

After tucking the Princess in bed, the Jester "went over to the
window and winked at the moon, for it seemed to the Court
Jester that the moon had winked at him".

The plot is simple and orderly, but in its development Thurber
is able to suggest many of the themes that exist in his other
work. The most important of these has to do with the function of
the self-conscious comedian as preserver of sanity in a chaotic
world. It is the clown who is best able to cope with a nonsensical
world, avoiding the dignified rigidity of the wise men (who must
protect their reputations for wisdom), and the anger which renders the king impotent at threats to his potency and authority.

Stylistically, *Many Moons* points toward what will become a
major source of comedy in later fairy tales. Beside the fantasy,
which we expect in a fairy tale, is a sprinkling of realistic detail
which forces the reader to acknowledge the reality on which
fantasy is based. Lenore had originally fallen ill "of a surfeit of
raspberry tarts"; "The Royal Physician came to see her and took
her temperature and felt her pulse and made her stick out her

tongue." And as each of the wise men is sent for, his statement of incapability is prefaced by a list of past accomplishments:

The Royal Wizard brought a long scroll of parchment from another pocket of his robe ... "Now let's see. I have squeezed blood out of turnips for you, and turnips out of blood. I have produced rabbits out of silk hats and silks hats out of rabbits ... I have made you my own special mixture of wolfbane, nightshade, and eagles' tears to ward off witches, demons, and things that go bump in the night ... horns from Elfland, sand from the Sandman, and gold from the rainbow. Also a spool of thread, a paper of needles, and a lump of beeswax – sorry, those are things my wife wrote down for me to get her."

The last sentence is funny precisely because it makes a man of the wizard. The trite wonders which precede it are juxtaposed with verbal tricks, suggesting that the wizard's real function is to amuse rather than assist the King – and the very wonders themselves are amusements. Since the wise men are really jesters, it is left to the Jester to be wise.

In *The Great Quillow* [8] the comic elements of *Many Moons* are even more successfully integrated. The hero is a toymaker in a little village which has been set upon by the giant, Hunder. The giant demands that the town support him, but this will bring about its economic collapse "within a week and a fortnight". The town council cannot devise a plan for getting rid of the giant, so everyone sets to work to fulfill the demands. One of these demands is that someone must tell Hunder a story which will amuse him, and since Quillow is the comedian, the task falls on him. Quillow's first tale is of a giant who had come in the past and had been afflicted " 'in the mind ... for the mind is a strange and intricate thing' ". The first symptom was a fifteen-minute period in which "all words were one word to him. All words were "woddly." The second symptom was that all the chimneys in the town appeared black, and the third was a sudden apparition in which the giant saw tiny blue men all around him. The giant scoffs at the story, but of course on the second day, Quillow, in the midst of another story, begins saying "woddly"

[8] *The Great Quillow* (New York, Harcourt, Brace and World, 1944). Copr. © 1944 James Thurber.

at the designated time. Everyone in the town says only this word
for the fifteen minutes and the giant is frightened. That night
Quillow has arranged for the chimney bricks to be painted black,
and the giant is so upset next morning that he agrees to fast all
day – thus sparing the town's food supply. On the third day,
Quillow had planted little blue men, which he had made for the
occasion, all around the giant, and when Hunder sees them he
runs to the ocean, the deepest waters of which, Quillow has told
him, are the only possible cure for his malady. Sometime later,
a traveler tells the villagers of a giant who has rushed into the
sea and drowned.

Stripped to its basic fable, *The Great Quillow* seems merely
another tale of a Giant outwitted by a Jack, in which children
can identify with the victory of small over large. Quillow seems
childlike in other respects also. He had no apparent concern over
his lack of dignity and enjoys amusing people:

It was the custom of Quillow's colleagues to shout merrily, "Why,
here comes the Great Quillow!" when the toymaker appeared. The
lamplighter or the tailor or the locksmith would sometimes creep up
behind him and pretend to wind a key in his back as if he were a
mechanical figure of his own devision. Quillow took all this in good
part, and always, when the imaginary key in his back was turned, he
would walk about stiff-legged, with jerky movements of his arms,
joining in the fun and increasing the laughter.

Nor is he indignant when the council members scoff at his plan
for getting rid of the giant, though they have no plan at all;
Quillow's acceptance of himself and his community is too secure
to be threatened by anyone else's scoffing. And in fact, it is
Quillow the clown who seems mature, and the giant who seems
childish. Hunder's demands on the town are those of an infant,
and in contrast to Quillow's his speeches seem infantile:

"[If your tales do not amuse me] I will put you in the palm of my
hand and blow you so far it will take men five days to find you. . . .
I can stamp upon the ground with my foot and empty a lake of its
water."

"I have no doubt of that, O Hunder," said Quillow, "for the thunder
is your plaything and the mountains are your stool. But the giant who
came over the hills and rivers many and many a year ago was a

lesser giant than Hunder. He was weak. He fell ill of a curious malady. He was forced to run to the ocean and bathe in the yellow waters, for only the yellow waters in the middle of the sea could cure the giant."

"Rowf," snarled Hunder, picking up another sheep. "That giant was a goose, that giant was a grasshopper. Hunder is never sick." The giant smote his chest and then his stomach mighty blows without flinching, to show how strong he was.

The relationship between Hunder and Quillow is one of child and parent; it is Quillow who is called upon to entertain the giant. Again, Thurber's story diverges from the normal fairy tale which supports the notion that imagination is a quality for children, one which is lost in maturity. Quillow's imagination sets him off from the rest of the villagers, but in his ability and willingness to deal with the otherwise insoluble problem posed by the giant, it is clear that his is the greatest maturity in the town. The mark of his maturity can perhaps best be seen in the passage which ends the story. After the traveler has brought the news of Hunder's drowning, the lamplighter repeats the tale to Quillow, who is making a new toy.

The lamplighter saw that the toy was a tiny replica of Quillow himself.

"What do you do with that?" he asked.

"You put it in the palm of your hand, like this," said Quillow, and he put the figure in the palm of his hand.

"And then you blow, like this." He blew, and the miniature Quillow floated slowly through the air and drifted gently to the floor. "I think it will amuse the children," said the little toymaker. "I got the idea from a giant."

Quillow's imagination provides him a view of the world in which he can comfortably see himself as a clown – even as a child's toy; his vision encompasses the figure of the giant whose shadow makes sightless the "practical" citizens. The shoemaker makes shoes, the lamplighter lights lamps, and Quillow makes marvelous, fanciful toys.

The principal difference between *Many Moons* and *The Great Quillow* is that the characters of the latter are developed more subtly and the style is more subdued. Where *Many Moons* abounded in verbal wit – sometimes merely for its own sake – the use of word tricks in *Quillow* is thoroughly integrated into the texture of the fable. And in *The White Deer*,[9] Thurber employs a style which is at once elevated, poetic, and comic, to suggest the "medieval" world of the story. The tone is solidly established in the opening paragraph:

If you should walk and wind and wander far enough on one of those afternoons in April when smoke goes down instead of up, and nearby things sound far away and far things near, you are more than likely to come at last to the enchanted forest that lies between the Moonstone Mines and the Centaurs Mountain. You'll know the woods when you are still a long way off by virtue of a fragrance you can never quite forget and never quite remember. And there'll be a distant bell that causes boys to run and laugh and girls to stand and tremble. If you pluck one of the ten thousand toadstools that grow in the emerald grass at the edge of the wonderful woods, it will feel as heavy as a hammer in your hand, but if you let it go it will sail away over the trees like a tiny parachute, trailing black and purple stars.

The magic and enchantment of this world is reflected in the alliterative and metrically rhythmic prose.

At times the prose becomes verse, as when King Clode tells to his three sons, Thag, Gallow, and Jorn, the tale of having chased a white deer in the enchanted forest with his own father and brothers. The deer, when cornered, became a beautiful princess who set perilous prothalamial tasks for Clode and his brothers; Clode won her hand. When he has finished the tale, a minstrel is announced:

"Then send him in, then send him in!" cried Clode. "He'll sing to us of strong men and the chase. I've had enough of sorrow and of love." (p. 11)

At times, the characters become conscious of their rhetoric. The minstrel tells Clode and his sons of another white deer, and since the chase is the king's principal occupation, he and his sons set out after it – Clode with some misgivings because he fears that another woman may intrude upon the man's world of the hunt. On the way they encounter a woods wizard:

"My father and my brothers and I pursued a deer," said Clode [to the wizard], "which against the wall of Centaurs Mountain underwent a marvelous and mortifying metamorphosis. I am a little touchy on the topic, too, so do not turn your tongue to taunts."

"He does not turn *his* tongue," said Jorn. "He twists your own, to 'm's' and 't's'."

"And 'w's'," said the wizard, "as you shall see."

"Try twice that trick on Tlode," said the King, with great dignity, "my mousey man of magic, and we will wid these wids of woozards." King Clode made a royal gesture of arrogance, authority and austerity, while his sons stared at him in astonishment. (p. 16)

In the fairy tale, as in none of the other forms he attempts, Thurber has found a means for integrating verbal skill with the themes which preoccupy him.

The fairy tale form, also, is uniquely suited for the investigation of appearance and reality which is the theme of *The White Deer.* This was also the theme of *Many Moons,* but its development is infinitely more subtle and complex in this novella-length later tale. Here there is no clown to symbolize the importance of imagination in an inscrutable world; instead, the hero is Jorn, the youngest prince, and the story is of his growth to maturity. The older brothers would perhaps be Babbitty businessmen in a "modern" story; their interest, like their father's, is in the chase. Jorn is a poet and a musician, but at the beginning he is also a romantic hero, in the Arthurian style. The deer that Clode and his sons chase becomes a princess, and in the manner of princesses, sets each of the sons a perilous labor. In performing their tasks, each of the princes is exposed to disillusionment appropriate to his values, so that, at the end, each of them could have come to a greater understanding of his world. Jorn, at the end, has learned something about the nature and values of both illusions and disillusionment; his romantic naiveté is replaced by conscious acceptance of necessary illusions.

The princess, into which the white deer is transformed, is unlike the usual victims of spells and sorcery. According to the Royal Recorder and Tocko, the clockmaker, such princesses can always remember their names and previous lives when they become human again. That this princess cannot reminds Tocko of one other such case his father had told him about, of a deer who was allowed to assume human shape because she had once saved the life of a woods wizard. This deer, so the story went, could retain her human form until love had failed her three times, at which point she would revert. King Clode and the Royal Recorder both assume that this must be the case with the present princess, but the King does not hear Tocko's story until the princes have left to perform their tasks. The story causes much concern and some amusement:

The Royal Recorder wondered if he could truly love a lady who might at this time or that, depending on the special spell that held her in enchantment, begin to nibble at the young leaves on the trees. He decided with a sigh and a shake of his head that he could not, and made a little note to this effect in the archives of his heart. (p. 30)

When the King hears the story, he is enraged:

"If I were King of all the world," said Clode, "I'd make an end of sorcery or break my backbone in the try. In such confusion and caprice, who knows his hound dog from his niece?" (p. 44)

But later Clode vows he would give half his kingdom " 'to see the face of Thag, the second huntsman of his time, waking to behold on the pillow next to his, the day the spell is broken, not raven locks and ruby lips but hairy ears and velvet nostrils!' "

The animal imagery in these passages is worth noting, for it reveals the polar attitudes which dominate most of the story's characters. In contrast to the romantic idealism with which the princess – in her human form – is viewed by all, is this opposing view – that woman is just animal. The two views are really one – the illusion, when shattered, simply reverses itself, but perception of the object is not enlarged. Tocko had once been Royal Astronomer, but he predicted the end of the earth so often that Clode fired him and hired a man who invented a rose-colored lens for his telescope. Clode wants to do away with all sorcery but this would deprive him of much in his world that amuses him, including his dwarf, Quondo. These dichotomies are revealed most amusingly in the monologue of the Royal Physician, when the latter is sick in bed:

"I'll never walk again. . . . Come, come, we'll have us out of bed in
no time; we'll bring the roses to those cheeks of ours in no time. . . .
No, we won't. . . . Yes, we will. . . . No, we won't. . . . Yes, we will."
    A long silence followed and the King entered the chamber. The
Royal Physician was taking his temperature, but he shook the mercury
down without looking at it.
    "As a physician, I must take my temperature every three hours,"
he said, "but as a patient, I must not be told what it is." (pp. 32-33)
[Thurber's ellipses.]

In his preference for the real over the imaginary, Clode depends
upon this physician to determine whether or not the princess is
a princess:

"The heart is much too high, *much* too high," [the physician] announced at last, "both as to location and rapidity of beat. There is a
skip, a definite skip, such as might be brought on by too much
leaping over brooks, *much* too much leaping over brooks, but I could
not give a final opinion, of course, until I had examined the brooks."
(p. 93)

The King, unhappy at this conclusion, would have much pre-
ferred to believe the "illusion" of the princess's humanity, yet the
party of "common-sense" to which he belongs is more susceptible
to plausible nonsense like the physician's, than to sorcery and
magic.
    The two older princes, like their father, scorn imagination and
fantasy, but their tasks lead them into confusion which their kind
of "reason" cannot resolve. Thag's path leads through a wondrous country in which he is beset by those who would encourage
him to enjoy life; but his single-minded pursuit of the Blue Boar
of Thedon Grove (in the Valley of Jeopardy) excludes all else.
The beast is asleep when Thag finds it and the prince kills with
neither anger nor pleasure. He races home, through pleasure and
peril, with no apparent thought of the princess or anything else:
another day, another dragon. Gallow's quest leads him after the
Seven Headed Dragon of Dragore, through the Forest of Willbe,
which might also have been called the Forest of Confidence-men.
By the time he reaches the dragon he has been bilked of almost

everything he owns. The dragon is a mechanical device in a carnival, and in order to win the Sacred Sword of Loralow, Gallow has to toss a ball into each of the dragon's mouths – which privilege costs him what remains of his fortune. He gallops home, determined and penniless, little wiser than his brother from his experience.

Jorn's labor was simplest of all, for the princess had immediately fallen in love with the youngest prince. All he has to do is pluck a thousand cherries from trees in a grove guarded by a clay and boxwood Mok-Mok, which everyone knows is covered by initials scratched there by children. He is disheartened by his bad luck and wishes that a task more "worthy of his strength and courage" had been set him. On his way, however, he meets a witch who is caught in a tree; as a favor for extricating her, she grants his wish – that his task be made harder. All Jorn can do about the Mok-mok is scare off a Roc perched on the monster's body; however, he discovers that he can pluck cherries from the tree only by counting to one thousand for each one. A little man appears suddenly who gives him a secret for picking the cherries, and by this time Jorn is willing to take a short-cut.

But no sooner has he picked his cherries than a huge black knight appears and challenges him. After a long battle, Jorn's sword finds a chink in the Black Knight's armor and the prince discovers, to his horror, that he has vanquished a "man of seventy years".

"I would not have fought so venerable a knight had I known," said Jorn.
   "You fought the fearful thing I seemed to be, and that's the test and proof of valor, that's the proof and test. When all is dark within the house, who knows the monster from the mouse." (p. 85)

The old man had once been set the same task as Jorn's, but upon discovering that the dreadful Mok-Mok was "this harmless thing of wood and clay" –

" 'Then love's a whim' I cried, 'and man's a fool!' . . . The peril and the labor, Prince, lie not in the dreadful monsters or in mighty deeds, but in the keeping of the heart a man has won. This is the Dolorous

Doom of one who rode not home to claim his lady's hand – that each Maytime till I die, I must be overthrown by love which once I overthrew." (p. 86)

The keeping of the heart entails acceptance of appearances, and this knowledge prepares Jorn for the greatest challenge of all when he arrives home.

The three princes have finished their labors and arrive home simultaneously; therefore, each presents himself to the princess in order of succession. But the princess has been told Tocko's story by this time, and insists on warning the princes before they make their choices. Both Thag and Gallow reject her, but Jorn accepts her as she is: " 'What you have been, you are not; and what you are, you will forever be.' " At this point, the princess, as it seems to Jorn, becomes more lovely than ever, and the dwarf, Quondo, is transformed into a Prince who happens to be the lady's brother. Both had been enchanted by a witch; the princess has been a princess all along. Jorn and the princess will live – not happily ever after – but with perhaps less than the usual amount of married bickering, since they have begun with a certain willingness to accept each other as neither base nor ideal. No one else in the story seems to have been changed by the revelation. Thag and Gallow are quarreling stupidly when we last see them, and the King is still threatening to do away with magic and wizardry.

The world of magic and wizardry, in which fables can exist, is well suited for the asking of such questions as we have seen Thurber pose. When the reader is not allowed to be certain about what is real and what is imaginary, his response imitates, in some measure, the responses of characters to the situations they face. The reader may tend to interpret everything in these stories symbolically, to lose touch with reality. One character looks for a box by which to circumscribe "the range of [his] anguish". The symbol leads him into fantasy, from which he emerges uncertain as to whether the cleaning-woman still lives, doubtful that things are going to get better instead of worse. Again, Mr. Preble's rebellion against his wife seems to occur in the symbolic terms of fantasy – terms which preclude either understanding or alteration of his real situation. In the fairy tales, where the relationship between the real and the imaginary is most deceptive, the conflicts, again, are between the realistic and symbolic apprehension of life. Prince Jorn's triumph is his dismissal of the ideals attached to romantic symbols and his acceptance of the realities of his "task" and his Princess:

The peril and the labor, Prince, lie not in the dreadful monsters or in mighty deeds, but in the keeping of the heart a man has won.

THE LIMITS OF COMEDY

In the years following the publication of *The White Deer,* a decline in Thurber's inventive powers occurred. Thurber himself mentions this in his *Paris Review* interview, in connection with two of his "autobiographical" books:

Well, *The Thurber Album* was written at a time [1948-1952] when in America there was a feeling of fear and suspicion. It's quite different from *My Life and Hard Times,* which was written earlier and is a funnier and better book. The *Album* was kind of an escape – going back to the Middle West of the last century and the beginning of this, when there wasn't this fear and hysteria. I wanted to write the story of some solid American characters, more or less as an example of how Americans started out and what they should go back to – to sanity and soundness and away from this jumpiness. It's hard to write humor in the mental weather we've had, and that's likely to take you into reminiscence. Your heart isn't in it to write anything funny. In the years 1950 to 1953 I did very few things, nor did they appear in *The New Yorker* ... the characteristic fear of the American writer is not so much [the mental climate] as it is the process of aging. ... Coupled with this fear of aging is the curious idea that the writer's inventiveness and ability will end in his fifties. And of course it often does. ... I once did a drawing of a man at his typewriter, you see, and all this crumpled paper is on the floor, and he's staring down in discouragement. "What's the matter," his wife is saying, "has your pen gleaned your teeming brain?"[1]

In addition to the bomb and to McCarthyism (which Thurber elsewhere blames for "the intimidation of writers and playwrights")[2] his own blindness must be taken into account when

[1] Malcolm Cowley, ed., *Writers at Work* (New York, Viking, 1957), p. 97.
[2] Thurber, "The Case for Comedy", in *Lanterns and Lances* (New York, Harper and Row, 1961), p. 42. Copr. © 1961 James Thurber.

considering the unevenness of his late work. At seven, in a child's game, Thurber lost one of his eyes, and the infection spread to the other eye before the afflicted one could be removed. For almost forty years he lived with extremely limited vision in one eye and by 1940 cataracts forced him to begin a series of five operations which led, on one hand, to "a nervous tailspin", and on another, to little more than gross perception of light and dark. By 1951 he was totally blind and so he remained until his death in 1961.

While this study makes no attempt to investigate Thurber's life, it is nonetheless difficult to ignore the effect that this blindness, in conjunction with a time of severe national tension, must have had upon his work. There is an increasing tendency in the later years to approach themes directly, where before, meaning had been allowed to emerge from concrete details. In his fables, Thurber found a way of controlling this inclination, for it is the nature of the form to make a direct statement with the barest illustration. Thurber told his interviewers, "I don't believe the writer should know too much where he's going. If he does, he runs into old man blueprint – old man propaganda." [3] And he was well advised. But Thurber's fables frequently avoid the blueprint insofar as they deny rather than affirm simplicity, pretending to do one thing, while actually saying another. Thurber's comedy at its best has always been devious; the masks we have seen him employ usually disguised the "blueprint" sufficiently for art to emerge.

In the later work, however, the masks are too often discarded. *The Thurber Album* (1952) is a collection of portraits of some of Thurber's nineteenth-century ancestors, professors he had known at Ohio State, and newspapermen he had worked for and with. In the passage quoted above Thurber described his wish, in this book, to return to "sanity and soundness and away from all this jumpiness". Some of the biographies are interesting, but there is little comedy, and the writing lingers somewhere between nostalgia and sentimentality. Thurber's imaginative essays have

[3]   Cowley, p. 87.

always depended for their artistic quality on digressive episodes which bring characters to life and incidents into sharp focus. But this talent is rarely evident in the *Album*. The blueprint is perhaps too apparent and the anger which kindles so much of the earlier work seems curiously restrained, as if the author feared losing control. For whatever reasons, it is a mediocre performance at best, and the author's own judgment seems to stand.

The Years with Ross (1959) is a different matter. Since it is essentially non-fictional, it lies outside the province of this study; however, it is outstanding journalism by any standards. One has only to compare it to Dale Kramer's *Ross and The New Yorker* to recognize the work of a first-class mind. It is the memoir Ford Madox Ford demanded, a picture of the time. Included are numerous sketches of writers and literary figures of the twenties, thirties, and forties. The sentimentality which spoils most of the *Album* is lacking here; instead there is warmth, comprehension, and above all, acceptance. The vision which sustained the early comedy operates throughout *Ross* though the effect is not so much of comedy as of memoirs by a comic artist. The book is anecdotal, but the masks by which Thurber previously transformed experience into comic art are not employed. The narrator emerges as a man similar to the figure described by the *Paris Review* interviewers.

Thurber's work had been to create a comic vision of the chaotic twenties and thirties, and in this, I believe, he was very successful. But even a vision as relatively confident as his was perhaps unable to endure a horror so large as the bomb. Early in his career he had warded off despair by acknowledging the inability of individuals to change external circumstances, and by urging acceptance of oneself and of the world. Perhaps youth and good health are necessary to such an acceptance. And perhaps things occur which simply cannot be accepted. In any case, Thurber, at the end, seems just too tired to be a clown any longer.

The advertisements in any issue of *The New Yorker* urge the reader to drink fine liquors, to fill his home with beautiful furniture, to dress his wife in "original" clothes, to attend the openings of Broadway shows, and to dine at the most elegant restaurants – in other words, to live as if he were wealthy and successful. The average *New Yorker* reader, however, is probably neither wealthy nor successful enough to indulge the tastes such advertisements would create. The average *New Yorker* reader is perhaps a man very much like the "little man" who appears so frequently in Thurber's stories: upper-middle-class, intelligent, financially secure (but not wealthy), on the way to success in his career (but not there yet), more or less happily married – a capable neurotic. The dilemma of this man is nicely represented by the demands made upon readers of the magazine. The fiction and journalism published therein are often of very high quality, requiring for comprehension and appreciation, a sensitive, liberal, intelligent reader. The advertisements, on the other hand, demand professional performance leading to material success, performance which in most modern endeavors is likely to be hindered by sensitivity and liberality – and some would add, by intelligence. Alas, a Ben Franklin still gets along better in our society than a Huck Finn.

The dilemma I describe is the same one documented at wearisome length by numerous commentators on contemporary American society. Every technological advance, every addition to man's knowledge or culture, makes a further demand upon the individual, who must, professionally, be a specialist, but who must also, culturally, despise specialization. Society expects a modern man to perform successfully in his career, and also to rule his home: to be a "good father" to his children, to repair defective machines, to be a satisfactory lover to his wife, and to attend plays and concerts with her. Not very much insight is needed to see that these requirements are greater than most of us can fulfill. The failure and frustration which must often result are reflected in the presently enormous demand for psycho-therapy. As Thurber seems to say, the humanity of modern man is defined by the eccentricities in which his frustrations become apparent.

Thurber's characters almost aways reflect the tension between the expectations society has of them and the incapacity of the demands for fulfillment. The result, as we have seen, is eccentricity. Occasionally, this appears as a psychosis, as with Mr. Bruhl or Mr. Barrett. More often the reaction is neurotic, as with Kinstrey, Andrews or Walter Mitty. The frustrations of these characters, however, take a significantly different form from that shown by eccentrics in the "autobiographical" stories. Thurber's grandfather and the Get-Ready Man were certainly as crazy as any of the modern neurotics, but Grandfather's madness had a quality of arrogant majesty missing in the later characters. The strongest impression the old man leaves with us is of indomitable vigor. He seems not to have been affected by the alienation which drives Walter Mitty into a fantasy world. Grandfather, like Lear, shouts his madness to the world; Mitty keeps his within and it threatens to destroy him. In David Riesman's *The Lonely Crowd,* the earlier "inner-directed" individual, who withstood alienation by asserting his integrity, is contrasted to the modern "other-directed" man, whose frustrations stem from his concern to be what others expect him to be. The distinction defines Thurber's characters as well as it does their models.

Occasionally, as we have seen, a "modern" character can achieve something resembling the integrity of his ancestors by becoming a self-conscious clown, by deliberately using comedy as a defense against frustration and anxiety. The most notable example of this is Tommy Turner, in *The Male Animal,* though the Thurber persona in the "autobiographical" tales also adopts this role. Although this is the most effective defense Thurber's characters can erect against their problems, it seems not to be transportable. The lesson must be relearned in every encounter; every situation must be met in a different way. Out of this constant need to redefine the tensions and their solvent, comes Thurber's art. No conflict can ever be permanently solved, no system or solution always works. Thurber's acceptance of the human animal's infinite variety forces him to approach his few basic situations in countless ways. The essence of his art is the importance of the concrete development of characters and situations, not the types of character or situation.

Thurber's comic representation of the dilemma of modern man is not unique. Most of the important British novelists of the period (1920-present) – Forster, Huxley, Waugh, Cary, Henry Green, and Anthony Powell – write from a vision substantially similar to Thurber's. James Hall's *The Tragic Comedians* demonstrates their use of eccentric upper-middle-class figures to represent the conflicts of modern life. Thurber, however, was the first writer, by a full generation, to render the American scene in terms of comic fiction. The other American comic writers of his time either directed their talents along non-fictional paths (White and Benchley), were rather superficial (Thorne Smith, Don Marquis, S. J. Perelman), or were content with the relatively easy victories of social satire (Sinclair Lewis, J. B. Cabell). Rarely does the tension which pervades Thurber's work appear in that of his comic contemporaries.

In the last few years, however, American writers have begun to follow the British lead. Salinger's ubiquitous *Catcher in the Rye,* Joseph Heller's *Catch-22,* Calder Willingham's *Eternal Fire,* Philip Roth's *Letting Go,* Bernard Malamud's *A New Life,* Saul Bellow's *Augie March* and *Herzog* – the list has grown almost long enough to call this a new wave in American fiction. In themes, characters, and sometimes in style, these books often seem similar enough to Thurber's work to nearly warrant suggestions regarding "influences". The curious reader might compare the scenes between Martha Regenhart and Gabe Wallach in *Letting Go* to the domestic quarrels of some of Thurber's characters; or the style of *Catch-22* to that in some of Thurber's "super-realistic" pieces. In any event, if these suggestions have any worth at all, they would have to be investigated in another study.

The time is too near Thurber's own to attempt any but the most tentative opinion regarding his ultimate stature in American literature. The case for Thurber must allow for the rather narrow scope of his vision, but it must also recognize that he sees very deeply into situations that interest him. T. S. Eliot has commented:

[Thurber's] is a form of humour which is also a way of saying something serious. Unlike so much humour, it is not merely a criticism of manners – that is, of the superficial aspects of society at a given moment – but something more profound. His writing and also his illustrations are capable of surviving the immediate environment and time out of which they spring. To some extent they will be a document of the age they belong to.[4]

In matters of style and technique, Thurber is, as I have tried to demonstrate, enormously accomplished; the apparent simplicity of much of his work should not obscure his virtuosity – rather it should be regarded as a testimony for it. I believe that Thurber, even more than Twain, is the finest comic artist that America has yet produced.

[4] Quoted in Cowley, p. 83.

BIBLIOGRAPHICAL NOTE

The footnotes to my text indicate specific debts to other critics, but I should like to mention here several books which I found helpful during my preparation of this study. In particular, James W. Hall's *The Tragic Comedians* (Bloomington, University of Indiana Press, 1963) suggested to me several concepts which led to insights about the nature of Thurber's work, and its relation to other twentieth-century comic writing. Of the several commentators on nineteenth-century American humor, three were especially useful; these were Walter Blair for his lengthy introduction to *Native American Humor* (San Francisco, Chandler, 1960), Kenneth S. Lynn, *Mark Twain and Southwestern Humor* (Boston, Houghton Mifflin, 1959), and Terence Martin, "Rip, Ichabod and the American Imagination," *American Literature* (September, 1959). Robert E. Morseberger's book, *James Thurber* (New York, Twayne, 1964) was printed some months after the basic work on this study had been completed; it contains an excellent bibliography.

BOOKS BY JAMES THURBER

The following is a list of the first American editions of Thurber's books. The list is arranged chronologically, according to the date of first publication. It is intended, not to be a bibliographical study in the proper sense, but rather to serve the reader who wishes to locate the principal collections of fiction, cartoons and essays.

(With E. B. White), *Is Sex Necessary?* (New York, Harper and Brothers, 1929).

The Owl in the Attic (New York, Harper and Brothers, 1931).

The Seal in the Bedroom (New York, Harper and Brothers, 1932).

My Life and Hard Times (New York, Harper and Brothers, 1933).

The Middle-Aged Man on the Flying Trapeze (New York, Harper and Brothers, 1935).

Let Your Mind Alone! (New York, Harper and Brothers, 1937).

The Last Flower (New York, Harper and Brothers, 1939).

(With Elliott Nugent), *The Male Animal* (New York, Random House, 1940).

My World – and Welcome to It (New York, Harcourt, Brace, 1942).

Fables for Our Time (New York, Harper and Brothers, 1943).

Many Moons (New York, Harcourt, Brace, 1943).

Men, Women and Dogs (New York, Harcourt, Brace, 1943).

The Great Quillow (New York, Harcourt, Brace, 1944).

The Thurber Carnival (New York, Harper and Brothers, 1945).

The White Deer (New York, Harcourt, Brace, 1945).

The Beast in Me and Other Animals (New York, Harcourt, Brace, 1948).

The 13 Clocks (New York, Simon and Schuster, 1952).

The Thurber Album (New York, Simon and Schuster, 1952).

Thurber's Dogs (New York, Simon and Schuster, 1952).

Thurber Country (New York, Simon and Schuster, 1955).

Further Fables for Our Time (New York, Simon and Schuster, 1955).

The Wonderful O (New York, Simon and Schuster, 1957).

Alarms and Diversions (New York, Harper and Brothers, 1957).

The Years with Ross (Boston, Atlantic-Little, Brown, 1959).

Lanterns and Lances (New York, Harper and Brothers, 1961).

Credos and Curios (New York, Harper and Row, 1962).

INDEX

STUDIES IN AMERICAN LITERATURE

1. JOHN BERNSTEIN: *Pacifism and Rebellion in the Writings of Herman Melville*. 1964. 232 pp.   ƒ 29.—

2. KARL F. KNIGHT: *The Poetry of John Crowe Ransom: A Study of Diction, Metaphor, and Symbol*. 1964. 133 pp.   ƒ 17.—

3. KENT G. GALLAGHER: *The Foreigner in Early American Drama*. A Study in Attitudes. 1966. 206 pp., Cloth.   ƒ 26.—

4. PAUL T. NOLAN: *Three Plays by J. W. (Capt. Jack) Crawford: An Experiment in Myth-Making*. 1966. 287 pp., portrait.   ƒ 32.50

5. NORMAN J. FEDDER: *The Influence of D. H. Lawrence on Tennessee Williams*. 1966. 131 pp. Cloth. ƒ 19.50

6. LEONARD GREENBAUM: *The Hound & Horn: The History of a Literary Quarterly*. 1966. 275 pp. 2 plates.   ƒ 32.50

7. KENNETH E. RICHARDSON: *Force and Faith in the Novels of William Faulkner*. 1967. 187 pp.   ƒ 23.—

8. CHESTER C. LONG: *The Role of Nemesis in the Structure of Selected Plays by Eugene O'Neill*. 1967. 230 pp.   ƒ 28.—

10. EDWARD M. HOLMES: *Faulkner's Twice-Told Tales: His Re-Use of His Material*. 1966. 118 pp.   ƒ 20.50

15. WILLIAM J. FREE: *The 'Columbian Magazine' and American Literary Nationalism*. 1968. 176 pp.   ƒ 26.—

16. JOHN D. BRANTLEY: *The Fiction of John Dos Passos.*
1967. 156 pp.   ƒ 21.—

17. GEORGE BRANDON SAUL: *Quintet: Essays on Five American Poets.* 1967. 50 pp.   ƒ 10.—

19. PHYLLIS FRANKLIN: *Show Thyself a Man: A Comparison of Benjamin Franklin and Cotton Mather.* 1969.
94 pp.   ƒ 21.—

20. JOSEPH J. WALDMEIR: *American Novels of the Second World War.* 1969. 180 pp.   ƒ 21.—

26. G. A. M. JANSSENS: *The American Literary Review: A Critical History 1920-1950.* 1968. 341 pp.   ƒ 38.—

MOUTON · PUBLISHERS · THE HAGUE